NAMES WERE CHANGED TO
PROTECT THE INNOCENT

Names Were Changed to Protect the Innocent

True Stories of a Police Dispatcher

Joseph L. Swick

Copyright © 2010 by Joseph L. Swick.

Library of Congress Control Number: 2010924537
ISBN: Hardcover   978-1-4500-6182-7
               Softcover   978-1-4500-6181-0
               Ebook   978-1-4500-6183-4

This book was printed in the United States of America.

Book cover designed by
Joseph L. Swick and Gary L Vincent/PHD

To order additional copies of this book, contact:
Xlibris Corporation
1-888-795-4274
www.Xlibris.com
Orders@Xlibris.com
77686

CONTENTS

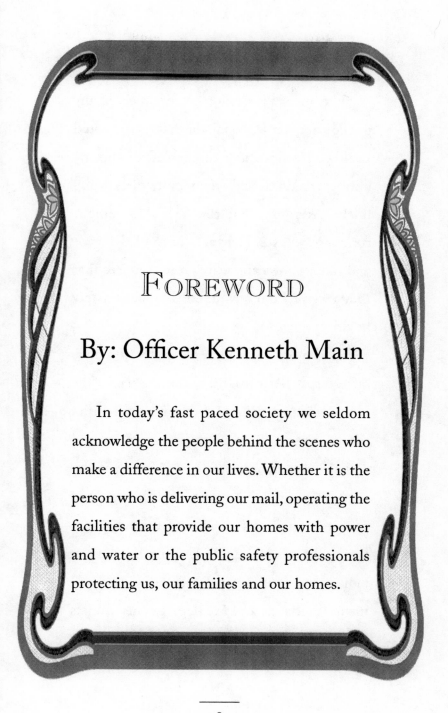

FOREWORD

By: Officer Kenneth Main

In today's fast paced society we seldom acknowledge the people behind the scenes who make a difference in our lives. Whether it is the person who is delivering our mail, operating the facilities that provide our homes with power and water or the public safety professionals protecting us, our families and our homes.

The life of a law enforcement officer or any public safety professional, for that matter could easily be classified as a miserable existence by normal standards and whats more dishearting is the citizenry that the law enforcement community serves. The public has high demands and rarely shows appreciation for services that they receive from anyone in the public safety field.

Even more rare is appreciation for the public safety dispatcher who is the on the other end of the phone when you call 911. In many communities the amount of calls received are numerous and and the dispatchers are few. This dispatcher must answer all these calls, sort through and prioritize them, log them and then dispatch them. All this while also keeping in constant radio contact with law enforcement, emergency medical services, and fire departments. Whats more is the public expects this all to be done in a professional manner twenty-four hours a day, 365 days a year.

In this book you will gain some insight into the public safety realm, by examining a number of real stories, many of which are humorous some of which are serious but all them are true. This book will help readers get an understanding of the daily life of a public safety professional and hopefully develop a certain level of understanding for their life and what they experience during their career.

You will find Joesph Swick's writing style personable and refreshing. Many times it feels as if he is speaking directly to you, in person. Furthermore I know you will appreciate the entertainment value of this book but please also take special note of the transformation in the law enforcement field described by Mr. Swick. By keeping this transformation in mind it's easy to understand the reasoning behind many trends in law enforcement.

In closing, I hope you enjoy this book and find it's contents as amusing and insightful as I have. Additionally, I think I speak for Mr. Swick when I say, please appreciate your public safety professionals and don't be afraid to show your appreciation for them whether that appreciation is demonstrated in a simple "thank you" in passing or in a formal letter written to that person's supervisor.

Officer Kenneth Main

THE

FID 🎻 LER

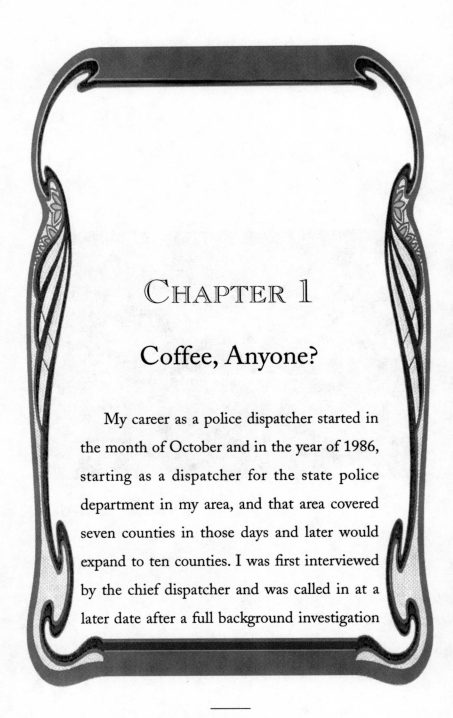

CHAPTER 1

Coffee, Anyone?

My career as a police dispatcher started in the month of October and in the year of 1986, starting as a dispatcher for the state police department in my area, and that area covered seven counties in those days and later would expand to ten counties. I was first interviewed by the chief dispatcher and was called in at a later date after a full background investigation was conducted, at which time I was interviewed by a captain who was in charge of the entire department, at which time I was offered the job as police dispatcher. After being informed of the job description and what all was expected of me, I was enlightened of the proper dress code. Dispatchers were not made to wear uniforms and were not allowed to have long hair below the ears, and no beards or long sideburns were allowed.

I had very little experience as a dispatcher, and I did have some business courses in college, typing, and some communication skills. From the headquarters we dispatched for seven counties and forty officers in our department and another twelve officers in the State Department of Natural Resources, known as the DNR, but most of the experience came from on-the-job.

I remember the first month of working on my own. I was working the day watch, and I went downstairs to the kitchen to get a cup of coffee and found there was none made. During that time, I was studying karate, and my instructor and his wife made great coffee, and they advised me that they put salt in their coffee to take away the bitterness, but what they had failed to tell me was how much salt! So I, not being at the department for very long, I wanted to make a good impression by making a great cup of coffee, so I put a great deal of salt in the coffee when I made it.

I went back upstairs to my cubicle while the coffee brewed, back to the radio and telephone and computer, and then later, after a few minutes, I went back downstairs to the kitchen to get me a cup of that great coffee I had just made. After pouring my coffee, I ran back up the stairs to the radio room, and I tasted the coffee for the first time, and it tasted just like saltwater. What to do next? I knew I had to go back downstairs to the kitchen and pour out the coffee and make more, but before I could do that, one of the officers came in with a fresh cup of the saltwater I had just made. I knew it had to be the same because we only had one coffeepot. But I knew he had not tasted it yet. This officer was a big guy and looked like a linebacker for the Raiders and was kind of scary to someone like myself who had not been there for very long. The officer, whom I will refer to as Officer Alpha, stuck out his big chin and looked out of the window and tasted the coffee/saltwater and made a face and shook his head. I guess he could not believe it tasted that bad because he took another drink and shook his head and mumbled, "This taste like saltwater." I was laughing inside but showed no emotion as he left the radio room with his saltwater. Needless to say, I did not admit to making that pot of coffee, and thank God no one saw me make that coffee.

It was probably seven or eight years down the road when that officer made first sergeant. And when Sergeant Alpha came into the office to collect money for the coffee fund, I finally told him about the time when I first started working for the department and made the coffee that tasted like saltwater, and he remembered that moment and time, and we now were able to have a good laugh. That was one of the happier moments I had with that agency.

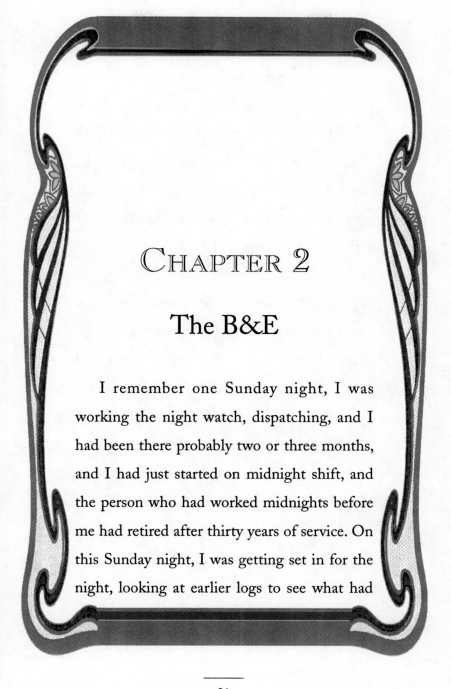

CHAPTER 2

The B&E

I remember one Sunday night, I was working the night watch, dispatching, and I had been there probably two or three months, and I had just started on midnight shift, and the person who had worked midnights before me had retired after thirty years of service. On this Sunday night, I was getting set in for the night, looking at earlier logs to see what had happened on prior shifts and waiting for the phones to start ringing, when I heard the sound of glass breaking from the building across from the police barracks, and I looked out of the window and saw a male subject holding what appeared to be a bar or pipe and breaking out a glass door. I gave out the information on the radio, and then I saw the subject carrying out several guitars through the broken glass door, and I gave out additional information to the officers (via radio), a description of vehicle and subject and direction of travel. After a long pursuit, an arrest was made. It was later found that the subject in question had a record and not been out of prison for very long. Also, I received three citations, one from the superintendent and two from the officers involved. Also, I made the front page of the local paper.

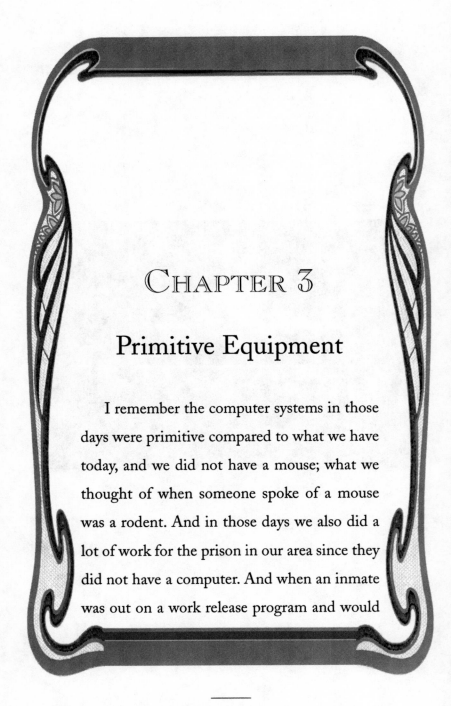

CHAPTER 3

Primitive Equipment

I remember the computer systems in those days were primitive compared to what we have today, and we did not have a mouse; what we thought of when someone spoke of a mouse was a rodent. And in those days we also did a lot of work for the prison in our area since they did not have a computer. And when an inmate was out on a work release program and would escape, our agency had to enter the subject in the law enforcement computer system and put out a Be on Lookout, or BOLO.

And nothing on the computer was preformatted, and you had to manually do everything and have every field in place or you would get rejected and you would have to start all over because nothing could be saved. And we had to look up every code in a thick Bible-print book and hope that after you pushed send, every tattoo and description was in the right field. We also had to enter stolen vehicles, articles, etc. while answering phones for the seven counties we worked.

Also, we had to hand-type everything when running a license check through DMV, and at that time, computers were down a lot, and we had to use microfilm to hand-check local registrations on vehicles and handwrite the information and give out the same (via radio) to the officer.

Later on we upgraded to another computer system, but still no mouse and nothing recorded in those days; the new upgrade had some things formatted, but we still had to look up codes and do manually most things that today would take seconds to do, and those days would take several minutes or hours to perform the same task.

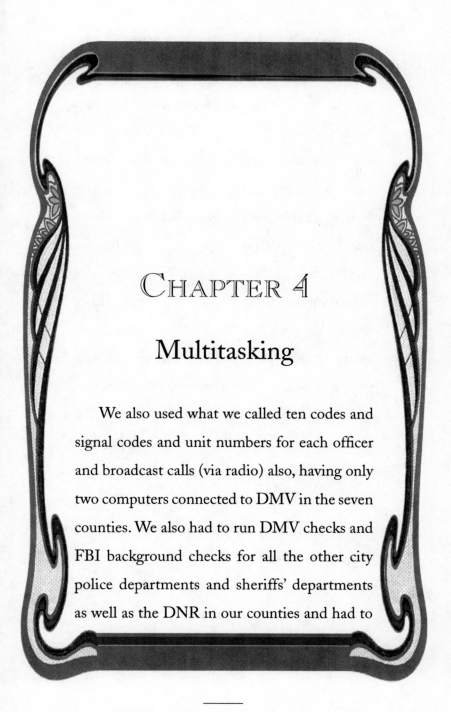

CHAPTER 4

Multitasking

We also used what we called ten codes and signal codes and unit numbers for each officer and broadcast calls (via radio) also, having only two computers connected to DMV in the seven counties. We also had to run DMV checks and FBI background checks for all the other city police departments and sheriffs' departments as well as the DNR in our counties and had to log each and every call by typewriter. We had to handwrite into a log all DMV checks, and any other information we ran and any radio traffic was logged on a typed log on an electric typewriter. And we had two different radio logs, one for the state police and the other for the DNR radio. At the end of the shift, we put the logged information on a binder after punching holes. Also, we had to file all incoming and outgoing teletypes. And radio traffic in those days was poor at best, and none of the officers had a handheld radio, so the only lifeline the officers had in those days was the dispatcher. After an officer arrived at the scene of a call, rule of thumb was to wait approximately fifteen minutes and then call the number from the original complainant; if no answer, try the car radio again, then if no answer, call out the next officer on call and send him to check on the officer. Fortunately, most of the time, the officer would be back into his car and would be okay before the responding officer got there. We had no cell phones, iPhones; we did have a fax machine, but in those days you had to pick up a telephone receiver and call like making a phone call and wait for another person to answer on the other end to fax information. So it was never used much, and if an officer was asked to call in by phone he went to a pay phone and gave us the number to call him.

CHAPTER 5

Respect

In those days the police officer had full authority and was respected by all, with the few exceptions, such as someone who was drunk, on drugs, etc.; but for the most part, whatever the officer put in his report was taken as the *bible*. And in those days they had no Mace pepper spray, and that's why the officers had to be a certain height and weight and great physical health, because when the officer responded to a call, more times than not, he would be alone and have no backup. And the dispatcher was his only lifeline, and a lot of the time, he had to use brute force to make an arrest because he had no Mace and was maybe dealing with more than one person. And sometimes they had to make a pit stop on the way to the jail to get someone sutured up and treated for injuries that had occurred during a fight they were in with one another or sustained by the officer making the arrest in defending himself. But we're talking about another age where the officer had no handheld radio, no pepper Mace, and the nearest backup was miles away.

When I first started in the department, I was told to screen all the calls because of the underfunding of the department, and most of the time we had officers on call on midnight due to the underfunding, and the dispatcher had to make sure that the call was a real call and something that could not be put off. I remember one time I called an officer out on a call. The officer was on call that night, and we'll call him Officer Beta. The caller advised that someone in a vehicle had struck part of the bridge on the highway, doing some minor damage to the bridge and leaving some of the car parts in the roadway. So me thinking that the vehicle may still be in the area and with a possible drunk driver, I called out Officer Beta, but he did not come out on the call. The next day I got called into the first sergeant's office, and we'll call him Sergeant Kappa. Sergeant Kappa asked me about the call in question, and I advised him that I did call out the on-call officer, Officer Beta, because I thought the vehicle might still be in the area and there was some property damage. He responded with his big finger in my face. "That's bullshit, you don't call anyone out on that type of call unless the vehicle is still in the area." Ironically, in later years, if I had not called out an officer on the same call or the same type of call, I would have gotten in trouble or fired.

So that's how things changed from the time I started working for that department up to the time I retired from that agency, and I lived through the transition from old school to new school, from a time where nothing was recorded or questioned to where almost everything was recorded and where everything was questioned. The transition was hard, but I conformed. We had people that would call in constantly when they were drunk, and some were mentally ill, and most of those calls were taken as a grain of salt due to the fact that we were underfunded and understaffed. And the laws were different from what they are today, and that has to be kept in mind when you hear some of these stories.

I remember one subject who called in a lot; we'll call him Mr. X. He called in on one full moon night, and he lived in a mobile home out of town, and I asked him what the problem was. He advised that he lived in a mobile home on a certain road and someone was trying to get into his residence. I asked, "Are they breaking in the door at this time and do you know who they are?" trying to obtain more information. And he went on to say that they were coming up through the floor of his mobile home, and I ask him, "How big is the hole in the floor?" And he answered, "About the size of a big rat hole." Needless to say, I did not call out an officer on that.

I remember another time, about 3:00 a.m. I heard on our scanner that the fire department in Mr. X's area was responding to a fire at his mobile home. And after about thirty minutes went by, I heard the fireman advise that they had been up and down that road where Mr. X lived and could not find any fire, and I then heard the fire dispatcher advise the fire department, "Mr. X will turn on his porch light to let you know which mobile home is on fire." I later called the other dispatcher and joked, "That must have been one hell of a mobile home fire if Mr. X had to leave on his porch light to let the fireman know where the fire was." But Mr. X would call in a lot and most of the time just talk about off-the-wall stuff, and if we would hang up on him, he would just call back; so most of the time, we would keep the line busy and pick it back up every fifteen minutes or so, and he would still be on the line, mumbling.

And speaking of Mr. X, when I first started in the police department, working for the first time on my own, at about 2:00 a.m., I received a call from Mr. X., who advised that someone was breaking into his residence, a mobile home on a certain road. And I called out the officer on call and was later balled out for doing so and was advised to never call out an officer when Mr. X called in because of all the false calls the subject had made and because he was nuts. But some years later, if I had not called out an officer on the same call, I would have gotten in trouble and written up. But this was a different time, and we had different laws and were working under a more restricted budget and were working with what would now be considered primitive equipment.

CHAPTER 6

Suicide

I remember an incident while working the evening shift early in my career. The caller was a mother, and her twenty-thee-year-old son was going through some type of depression and was threatening suicide and was sitting outside on the steps with a .44 Magnum pistol to his head. I dispatched two officers to the call and kept her on the phone,

That had to be the worst place for an officer to go into because if a person would take his or her own life, they would not think twice about taking someone else with them. Meanwhile, on the phone, the subject's mother kept telling me, "He's gonna do it, he's gonna do it, he's raising the gun." And at any time, I kept waiting to hear gunfire, knowing either the subject had shot himself or one of the officers shot him in self-defense, and I would have to have called the emergency squad. But after about twenty minutes, the subject put down the gun, and the ordeal was over, and the subject was taken into custody without incident.

There is a great deal of pressure on a dispatcher when put into these types of situations, but you have to remain calm and not get caught up in the moment because if a dispatcher panics, he is of very little help, if any, to the officers involved. And in the early days that was really important because we were the only lifeline the officers had. Also, the officers had a lot of respect for the dispatchers, and we had a lot of respect for the officers because they put their lives in our hands, and not just anyone could be put in that position.

With just about every call we had, the officer that was higher up would stand behind us in most cases because they knew we did the best possible job a person put into that position could do because we had to prioritize all the calls coming in and going out. And sometimes, out of the seven counties, we would have two or more wrecks and possibly a domestic, and the phones would be ringing off the hook at the same time.

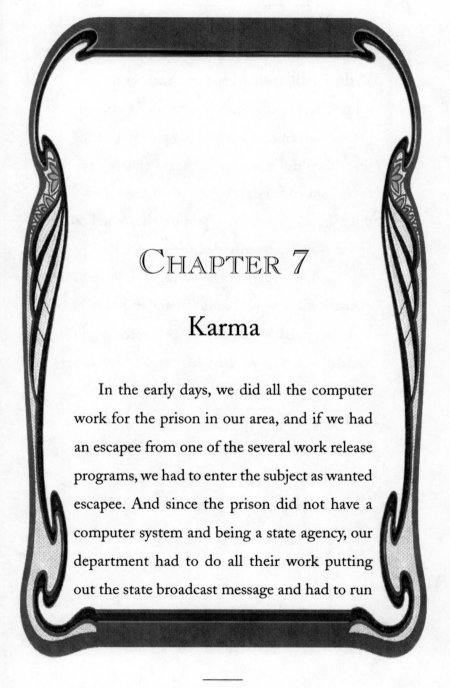

CHAPTER 7

Karma

In the early days, we did all the computer work for the prison in our area, and if we had an escapee from one of the several work release programs, we had to enter the subject as wanted escapee. And since the prison did not have a computer system and being a state agency, our department had to do all their work putting out the state broadcast message and had to run all the DMV and FBI and criminal checks and wanted and stolen property entries for each of the local seven counties and city police agencies since they did not have a computer terminal. So it kept us very busy. But that's the way we did things in those days because all the police agencies were underfunded.

Another thing, in the early days, we had camaraderie among the officers and dispatchers and hospitals and all the other agencies; you might even say we had karma. To give an example, if the officers didn't mess with you in some form of a practical joke, then you probably were not liked very much; so it seemed like we were always joking around with one another when we were not busy.

Here's another story I remember we had an officer who lived at the police barracks, where the department had rooms upstairs, and we'll call him

Officer Delta. The barracks walls were painted concrete blocks, and they had this large metal garbage can upstairs in the hallway, and Officer Delta always liked playing jokes on the new officers who stayed in one of the rooms after just coming out of the police academy. He would wait until the new officers had been there for about a week or two, and around 2:00 or 3:00 a.m., he would take the lid off the metal can and throw it down the hallway, making it bounce off the sides of the wall and waking up the new officers, laughing all the while.

One time we had two new officers fresh out of the academy staying in one of the rooms, and at around 2:00 a.m., Officer Delta threw the lid down the hallway, making a lot of noise as the lid banged off the side of the walls; and one of the new officers came out of the room in his underwear with his service revolver drawn and hammer pulled back, and that ended the throwing of the lid in the future.

Another story involving Officer Delta is that he liked to play practical jokes on the evening dispatcher. I remember that one evening, Officer Delta and other officers told the evening dispatcher that they had been receiving a lot of threats involving people who were mad at the police and to take all calls on that subject seriously. And at the same time, setting the dispatcher up for a practical joke. So Officer Delta, after priming the dispatcher, waited about twenty minutes and then sneaked around the side of the building and put an M-80 firecracker in between the window and the air conditioner and lit it. And I was told later that the dispatcher wet his pants and got down on the floor when the firecracker went off. They messed with each other all the time and all in good faith.

I remember one time when a dispatcher messed with one of the officers by putting a smoke bomb that hooked up to the car battery in his cruiser and just put off a lot of smoke a few seconds after the vehicle was started. The dispatcher gave the officer a false call, and when that officer ran out and started his cruiser, it started smoking from under the hood, and the officer called in on his radio, requesting the dispatcher to call out the mechanic to look at his engine that he thought had just blown up. And after letting the officer stew for a few minutes, he told him it was just smoke and was a prank.

Like I've said before, if you didn't have a joke played on you or if you didn't joke with someone else, then you probably weren't well liked in those days. And of course, later on in years, you would have probably been suspended or lost your job for doing the same joke.

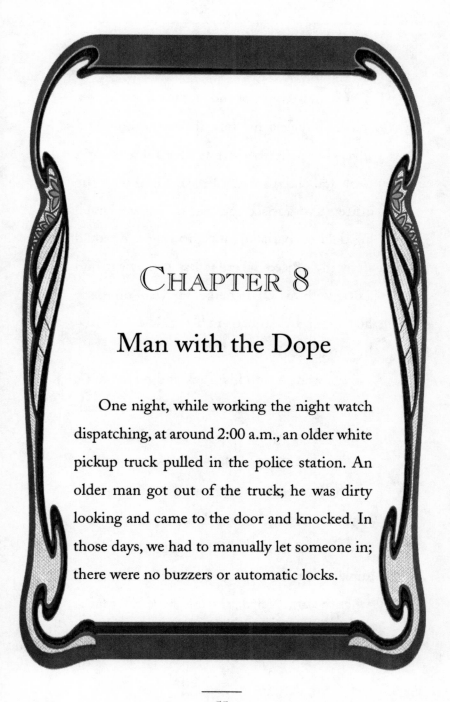

CHAPTER 8

Man with the Dope

One night, while working the night watch dispatching, at around 2:00 a.m., an older white pickup truck pulled in the police station. An older man got out of the truck; he was dirty looking and came to the door and knocked. In those days, we had to manually let someone in; there were no buzzers or automatic locks.

I went to the door and let the subject inside, and he followed me into the radio room and advised that he was arrested for DUI about a week ago and wanted to make a deal with the officers and advised me that he knew where a big field of marijuana was growing and would show the officers where it was if they cut him a deal with his DUI charge. He went on to say he had some marijuana in his vehicle. I advised him to go get it.

He went out to his truck and pulled out a six-foot stock with about one thousand seeds on it and brought it into the office. I called the undercover officer and let him know what I had, and he had me tag it with a piece of paper and advised me to get subject's name, address, and phone number and he would get back with the subject in the morning. I advised the man of what the officer had said, and he left. As far as

I know, the officers did not make any deal with the subject, and I never heard from him or any more about it.

One other night, I was working dispatch, and I received a call from a custodian who had just finished cleaning up at a supermarket that was adjoined to a drugstore. He advised me that while he was locking up and getting ready to leave, a man came down through the ceiling onto the floor of the supermarket after entering through the store roof, but the man did not see him, and he then called the police.

So I notified the officer on call, Officer Sigma, and when the officer got to the scene, he saw the suspect carrying what appeared to be a weapon and, aiming his 12 gauge shotgun at the subject, advised him to drop the weapon or he would be shot. The man did and was arrested without incident. Later, the officer came into the office and laid the weapon down. It was a stick of pepperoni that the subject had grabbed while in the store and almost got shot. Also, the man advised the officer that he was supposed to have dropped into the drugstore, not the supermarket.

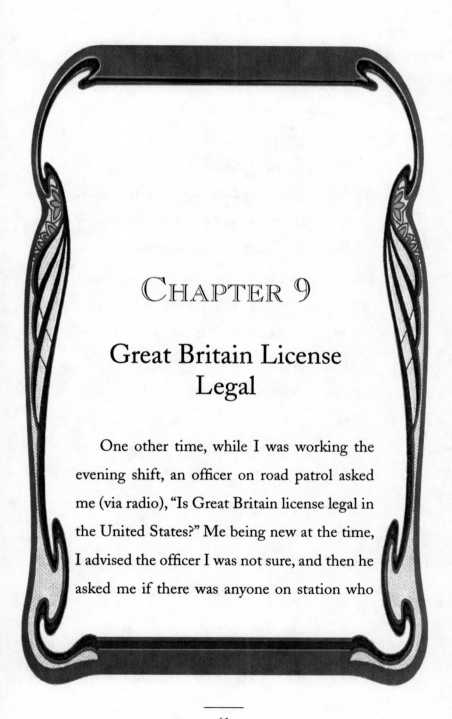

Chapter 9

Great Britain License Legal

One other time, while I was working the evening shift, an officer on road patrol asked me (via radio), "Is Great Britain license legal in the United States?" Me being new at the time, I advised the officer I was not sure, and then he asked me if there was anyone on station who might know. I advised him that Sergeant Alpha was on station and I would ask him.

While I was walking toward Sergeant Alpha's office, I was laughing because I knew he was so laid-back and knew what his answer might be. So I walked into Sergeant Alpha's office and explained to him that the other officer had a subject stopped on the four-lane and wanted to know if Great Britain license was legal in the United States.

He, as before, stuck out his chin and said, "Great Britain license? Does he have that guy stopped?" I advised yes, and he said, "Tell him to let that subject go." I took it from his answer that he didn't know either, but I advised the officer of that (via radio), and then I had to laugh. Later, the officer who had the subject stopped advised me that the subject was from Canada and he wrote him a DMV citation but didn't know if the subject had diplomatic immunity or not.

One night two police officers were dispatched to a two-story house out in the middle of nowhere because someone was supposed to be throwing rocks or something through the upstairs windows. When the officers got to the scene, they were talking to the owner when they heard glass breaking from the back of house. They walked all around and never saw anyone on this clear, full moon-lit night, and while on that side of the house, they heard glass breaking from the front side of the house.

After not seeing anyone outside the residence, one officer advised the other officer to take the cruiser and leave, and he would go upstairs in the house to look outside from the upstairs window and see if he could find out who was doing this, and the other officer left. The other officer who stayed behind went upstairs in the house and was looking out of the window. After about five minutes, he heard glass breaking in the other room. When he investigated, he found that the owner's little boy had a hammer in his hand and had been running back and forth from room to room, breaking the glass out.

CHAPTER 10

Flying Saucers

One night about 3:00 a.m., I received a call from the fire department, and they advised that they were in pursuit of a strange light in the sky and wanted an officer to go with them. I advised the officer on call that the fire department was pursuing a strange light in the sky and all night thinking they were getting closer but really never seemed to be getting anywhere near it.

They were out all night, until daybreak came and they could no longer see the bright light, and they ended the pursuit, and to this day, no one knows what it was.

One other time I had planned to go on vacation, and we were to leave on Saturday, but the night before, on Friday, when I came into work, Officer Delta and another officer told me to check my mailbox. After doing so, I found some papers that stated that my vacation had been canceled due to the fact that another dispatcher who worked at the other department over one hundred miles away was having a cancer operation and would be off work for some time, and I would have to report to that agency on Monday.

After calling my girlfriend, who was going with me on vacation, and telling her that my vacation had been canceled and that I was being transferred to another agency, she was upset and crying. I explained to Officer Delta that I was going to call Captain Omega, whom I was good friends with, at nine in the morning and find out why the short notice on the cancelation. Since they had known about the other dispatcher's operation for about two months, to cancel my vacation with one day's notice didn't seem fair. After letting me stew for about two hours, Officer Delta advised that it was a joke and I was not being transferred and that my leave was not canceled and that the state seal was not on the leave papers. So I called my girlfriend back, and everything was great again, and we went on vacation and had a good time.

One other time, I remember while working the night watch dispatching, I took a call around 4:00 a.m., and it was a little girl on the phone, and she was calling from another neighboring state. At that time, phone calls were very expensive, and at that time we did not have caller ID and it was hard for calls to be traced. She advised me where she lived and that she was only eight years old and was in the house alone with her six-month-old brother.

I kept her on hold after obtaining her grandmother's phone number from her, and I called and left a message on their machine as to what was going on and to call me as soon as possible. I also notified the authorities in the state where she lived. And after about twenty minutes on the phone with the little girl, I went back to the phone again, and a lady came on the phone and wanted to know who I was. I advised her that the little girl called the police and that our department was about one hundred miles away and was advised that she was at home alone with her little brother. The lady advised me that she was the child's mother and that the child liked playing with the phone and that her and her husband had been sleeping and just woke up.

I advised the lady that I had contacted the authorities in her area and called and left a message on the grandmother's answering machine and not to let her little girl play with the phone. I don't know what happened after the authorities got involved, and they never contacted me back, and I'm not sure if the mother's story was the truth or if the little girl was alone with her little brother.

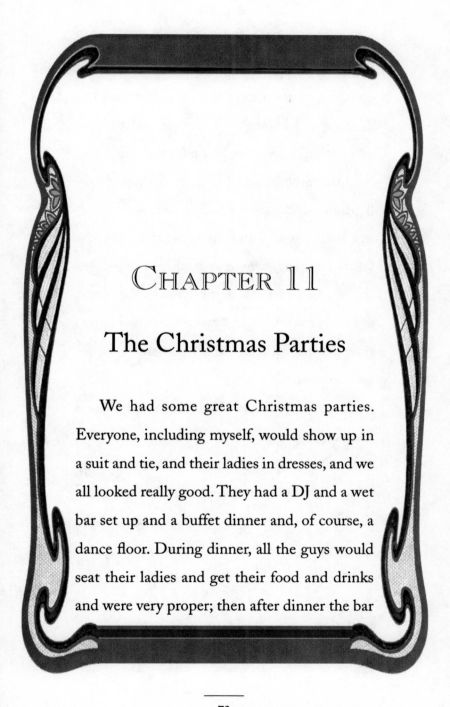

CHAPTER 11

The Christmas Parties

We had some great Christmas parties. Everyone, including myself, would show up in a suit and tie, and their ladies in dresses, and we all looked really good. They had a DJ and a wet bar set up and a buffet dinner and, of course, a dance floor. During dinner, all the guys would seat their ladies and get their food and drinks and were very proper; then after dinner the bar opened and the music started and we started dancing and having a great time and the ties came off and everyone let down their hair.

Just remember, after a year of working hard and dealing with people and not getting out much, we all looked forward to the big Christmas party, where we could get away from the work area for one night. Even though most got plastered one night a year, we still had a great time dancing and talking with others whom we had not seen for a while.

I remember one Christmas party when I brought my girlfriend with me, and after dinner I had more than a good time, filling up my drinking glass at every table, hence BYOB. And I would stop to mingle, and at one point, the drink was so strong, I had to add sugar to finish the drink. And later while on the dance floor, the boilermaker was taking its toll, so I had to run to the restroom to vomit. And the captain's wife was plastered as well.

The next year, at the Christmas party after dinner, First Sergeant Alpha made an announcement. "We have a winner for last year's Party Animal of the Year Award. The award goes to Joseph L. Swick." So I went up to accept the award—a plaque with a gold horse's ass on it, which I still have.

And meanwhile, the captain's wife was clapping her hands at her table when Sergeant Alpha advised, "We also have another winner, the captain's wife." And her hand clapping ceased as she made her way up to receive her horse's-ass award for Party Animal of the Year. She advised me later that she put hers on her desk at work, and mine is still hanging on the wall.

At one of the last Christmas parties I remembered, again all the officers and coworkers came with their husbands, wives, and girlfriends, all decked out in suits and dresses. And again, all the guys were gentlemen until dinner was over and the wet bar opened and the music started. Next I looked all around, and some of the officers had their shirts opened and their neckties around their heads and were on the dance floor and having a good time letting their hair down. Being in law enforcement, they never got to do that very much, so it was great to see that everyone was having a good time.

I remember one of the officers was getting a little bit intoxicated and having a good time a big guy, and he went over to the Christmas scene by the window of the building we had rented for the party and picked up a plastic camel and put it across his back and walked around with it and later put it back. But everything was in good taste, and all had a good time and we all got along.

And that night, twelve of us, including myself, were given a number, one through twelve, and then we were called up number by number in front by Sergeant Alpha. And then with the numbers, we were advised, we were going to sing the "Twelve Days of Christmas," and when our number would come up, we were to sing that verse for the number we had received. Some could not carry a tune, and what they didn't know was I was a singer, so I didn't mind at all.

I really looked forward to the Christmas parties which the department had, from the time I started in 1986 till they stopped having them in 1997. Also, Christmastime during work, a lot of companies would bring in fruit baskets and candy and homemade cookies. And about two weeks before Christmas, other companies would bring in a box of candies and a wallet for every worker in our department. And in the early years, we would get a bottle of Jack Daniel's, and if you didn't want it, you could give it to someone else, and that stopped about the time the Christmas parties stopped. It's like everything was changing from old to new, and some of the old ways, I missed.

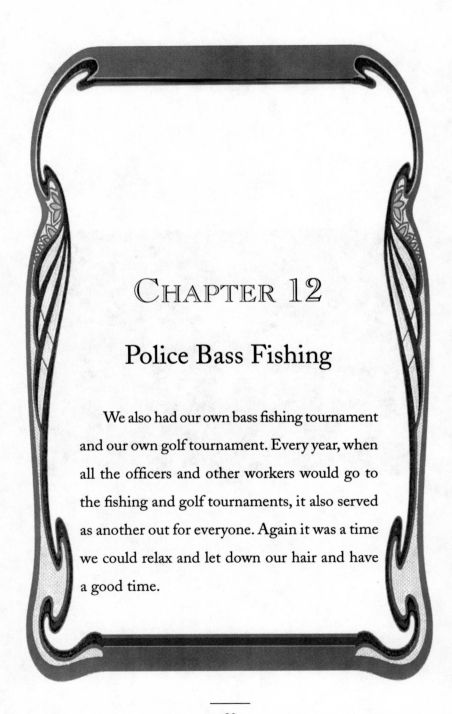

Chapter 12

Police Bass Fishing

We also had our own bass fishing tournament and our own golf tournament. Every year, when all the officers and other workers would go to the fishing and golf tournaments, it also served as another out for everyone. Again it was a time we could relax and let down our hair and have a good time.

We had two person per boat and had somewhere between forty and fifty boat entries, and we would start at around 7:00 a.m. and go till 4:00 p.m., and all fish caught were placed in a live well on our boats and brought in and measured and weighed and booked and set free back into the water.

The tournament lasted for three days, and we had to stay in a hotel for two nights. I remember the first time I went to the bass fishing tournament, me and another dispatcher who had fought for the right for non-police officers to go. I had never fished for bass from a boat before, but I had trout fished, so the first day at the tournament, I showed up wearing hip rubber boots and a trout vest and a creel, and some of the guys got a laugh out of that.

The other dispatcher had a bass boat, and on the first day, we were doing fairly well when he yelled, "Get the net! Get the net! I have a whopper on the line." I got the net, and he had hooked a big turtle. But we still finished twelfth out of forty-seven boats, and that's not so bad for a first timer.

At another bass fishing tournament, we stayed in the hotel across a karaoke bar, and we walked to the bar after we brought our boat back to the hotel and showered. And we all were intoxicated and singing karaoke and shooting pool, and we all got along great and closed the bar that night. Some made it on time at the lake the next morning, and some of us showed up a little late because of the nightlife at the bar. And that's another time I looked forward to up until the time I retired.

Another time during a bass fishing trip, Officer Gamma and his fishing buddy was out on the lake and pulled the boat to the side of the lake bank, and while getting off the boat, Officer Gamma had one foot on the boat and the other foot on a rock, and the boat moved spreading out his legs so far, he fell into the water. His buddy advised that he was laughing until he looked at his fish finder and found they were in ninety-three feet of water. He later came back to the dock, wet, and had changed into his rain suit since his clothes got wet.

Another time, I was fishing with Officer Tau, and he was using a very expensive lure, and we were in about fifteen feet of water, and he hooked his lure on a log and tried to retrieve it by pulling on it until it broke. He explained that he was a great swimmer and was going in after it. He took off his shoes and shirt and dived into the lake and went down about three times and came up empty. And I'm thinking, "He's going to get his finger caught in one of the barbs on the hook and tear his finger off when he has to come up to breath." But he stopped trying, and we left the cove and went somewhere else on the lake to fish.

Another time, I was fishing with Officer Rho, and after the first day of fishing, we had eaten dinner at the hotel where we were staying. We decided to go out and run around in town for a while, and several other officers saw us leaving at around 7:00 p.m., and after a few hours, we came back to the hotel; it was 11:00 p.m. And I told Officer Rho I was going up to the room and try to get some sleep since we had to be on the water at seven the next morning. I set the sleep timer on the TV and turned to a channel I liked and went to sleep.

At around 5:00 a.m., Officer Rho came into the room and had been drinking and said, "You won't believe what me and some other officers did. We moved everyone's boat to another location in the hotel lot, and they will wonder what happed to their boats in the morning."

I was mad at him, and I told him they should not have done that because some of those boats are these people's lives and are very expensive. I was being blamed for being involved by association until Officer Rho explained I had nothing to do with it.

CHAPTER 13

Horsepower

One night, at around 1:30 a.m., I dispatched an officer to a vehicle accident where some horses were in the road and had been struck by some vehicles. They were six horses that had gotten onto the four-lane highway, and all were struck by three vehicles at high speed. When the officer arrived at the scene, he saw a lady still in her Lincoln Town Car; and she was crying, not because she was hurt, but because she had a full-size horse lying across the hood of her vehicle and was dead. Three other horses had to be put down; all told, all six horses had died, but there were no injuries to any of the drivers, and they had to bring a tow truck to move the horses out of the road way.

I remember one other call at around 3:00 a.m. from a lady who advised that someone was fooling around outside her residence, and she was there by herself, and she lived about twenty-five minutes away from the office. I dispatched two officers, who responded in two different cruisers, and when they arrived at the scene, there were about two inches of snow on the ground, and they both looked all around the area and never saw any tracks in the snow. So if someone was fooling around outside her residence, they had to be flying. The officers approached the residence, and to their surprise, the lady's husband answered the door, and the officers explained about the call from the lady of the house, and the man advised the officers that he was her husband and had been sleeping on the couch and no one was fooling around outside, and his wife was nuts. The officers left the area; hence another case where officers risked their lives responding to a false call.

CHAPTER 14

World's Dumbest Criminals

There was one time when an officer was walking his beat downtown on a full moon-lit night, and the officer looked up at a third-story window, and there was a man dressed in all black, trying to break into the third floor of a residence. The officer pulled his service revolver and yelled at the suspect to show his hands; and the suspect, who was holding on with his hands, fell like a rock onto the sidewalk three stories below, landing close enough to the officer to tear off his tie clip, and the officer called for the emergency squad, and the subject was taken to the hospital and spent the night for observation for minor injuries and was released the next day to start serving time in the county jail. It was later learned that the suspect had been in and out of prison for burglary. I always said, "If that had been some poor worker, painting, and had fallen from that high, he would probably be dead."

Another time, we had three different officers out in different vehicles, and a subject was fleeing from one of the officers after flashing lights and siren were activated. And the officer called in pursuit—and that's something no dispatcher likes to hear—after going down different streets and onto the main highway, and at this time, all three officers were involved in the pursuit. After about five minutes into the pursuit, the suspect decided to take a shortcut, and one officer followed him, and the others went to where they knew the shortcut came out to head him off. And the other officers got at the intersection in ample time to put out the stop spikes. But while trying to remove the stop spikes from the canvas bag, the officer was unable to get them out of the bag, tearing and pulling at the bag while the pursued vehicle went on by, with the other officer on his tail. Fortunately, there was a county unit ahead and set up a roadblock, and the subject was apprehended.

One other story I remember, there was a local bank robbery, and at the time, they had very little information on the suspects, other than it was a white male wearing a dark mask and had a handgun and was wearing gloves and left in a dark-colored van in a unknown direction of travel. And they got away with approximately thirty thousand in cash, until one of the suspects contacted his sister in another state and told her he had just come into a lot of cash and wanted her to hold it for a while and he would later split it with her. But what he didn't know was that she was more honest than he knew; she contacted authorities, and when the officers went to the subject's residence and walked by the black van and entered his residence, they were amazed to find a drawing of the bank outlined on the coffee table into the wood. And the route they would take. Needless to say, the subject was arrested and was sentenced to ten years in prison.

I remember early in my career receiving a call around 2:00 a.m. on a Saturday night of a fight at a bar. I advised Officer Delta, who responded alone and with no handheld radio or pepper gas.

Also earlier that day we had a report of a stolen vehicle, so when the officer arrived at the scene of the fight at the bar, he saw the stolen vehicle in the bar parking lot and parked his cruiser behind the stolen vehicle and went into the bar alone. And after going inside, he found four subjects fighting, and he advised them, "Break it up, this is the police." And everyone stopped fighting except the subject who had stolen the vehicle, and after breaking up the fight, the officer arrested both those subjects and called for a tow truck for the stolen vehicle and made a pit stop at the hospital for treatment of the suspects who were injured either in the fight or by the officer using force to make an arrest and later taken to the county jail. One subject was arrested for grand larceny, and the other subject was arrested for obstructing.

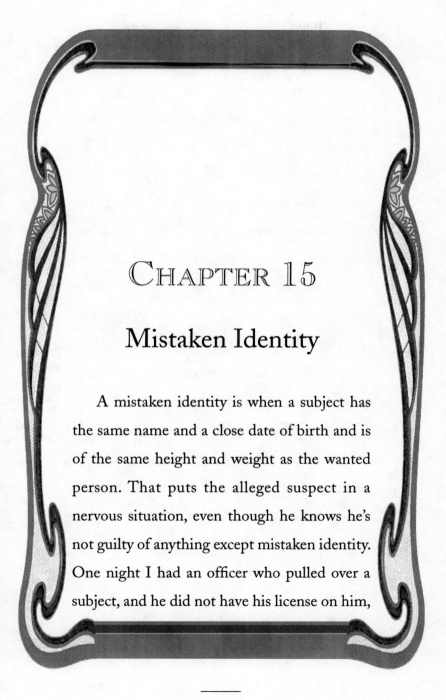

CHAPTER 15

Mistaken Identity

A mistaken identity is when a subject has the same name and a close date of birth and is of the same height and weight as the wanted person. That puts the alleged suspect in a nervous situation, even though he knows he's not guilty of anything except mistaken identity. One night I had an officer who pulled over a subject, and he did not have his license on him, and he advised the officer that he had left it at home. The officer ran the subject's name and date of birth; it came back as a wanted person for murder in another state, with a close date of birth, and height and weight were close, and hair color was the same. As I was giving out the information on the wanted subject, and the alleged suspect was sitting beside the officer in the cruiser, according to the officer who was there, the subject had turned about three different shades of color and told the said officer that he had never been in any trouble in his life. And the subject was right, and he was released. I could only wonder what was going through that guy's head, but the officer was in the right and had to check the subject out.

Another case of mistaken identity was when we had a bank robbery in another county, and fifteen thousand dollars was taken, and the officers were looking for someone who didn't have a lot of money but who now was throwing money around. The next night, while at a local bar, a male subject was throwing around one-hundred-dollar bills and buying other people drinks, and someone at the bar called the authorities, and an officer was dispatched, and when they interviewed the subject, he explained he had taken out a bank loan on his house because he was going through a divorce and he wanted to get as much money as he could before that took place, and the man produced the information to the officers that confirmed that he did take out a loan on his house for fifteen thousand dollars, and the subject was released.

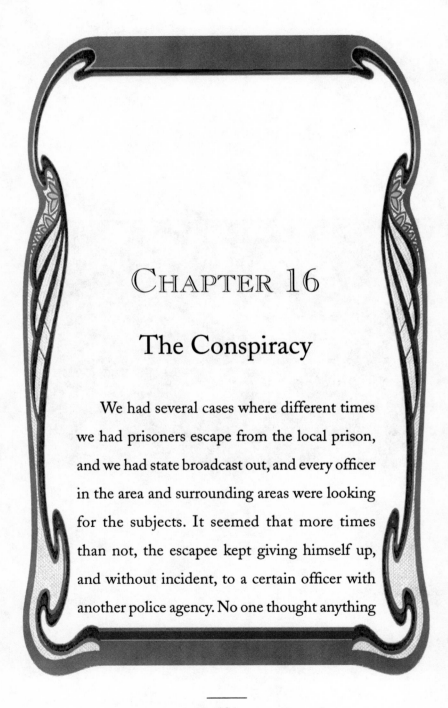

Chapter 16

The Conspiracy

We had several cases where different times we had prisoners escape from the local prison, and we had state broadcast out, and every officer in the area and surrounding areas were looking for the subjects. It seemed that more times than not, the escapee kept giving himself up, and without incident, to a certain officer with another police agency. No one thought anything about it until someone advised that the officer was spreading around that if the other police agencies would catch up with the prisoner or prisoners, they would be shot on the spot with no questions asked. However that statement was never proven, but it did cause some hard feelings between the different agencies.

I remember one night while I was working the midnight watch, I received a call from a male subject who advised that he approached some lady on the side of the highway who advised she was out of gas in her car about five miles west of the police office. I notified the officer, who went to the mechanics room and took a gas can and filled it up and proceeded to the subject's location, and when he got to the scene, he found that the lady was praying. The officer advised her that he had brought fuel for her vehicle; she advised him she did not need his help, that God was sending her help from her sister, and the officer advised her he would leave but he would have to tow the vehicle if it was still there in the morning. And the officer left, and later the officer advised me she was praying to God for help and he sent it, but she was too dumb to see it.

While working on evening shift, on a nice afternoon, and at around 4:00 p.m., I had a male subject stop by the office, and he looked deranged and was yelling, and when I looked out of my window from the radio room, he was stating he was going to kill himself. He had what looked like a knife up to his throat and advised he was having some family problems and was going to kill himself.

I notified the officer to come into the office ASAP, and I advised the subject that someone was coming to speak with him, and I tried to talk him down, and not being experienced in that field, I did the best I could until the officer came on station. And after a few seconds, which seemed like an hour, and I'm thinking, "Anytime, this guy is going to kill himself or maybe throw the weapon at me," the officer came on station, and after talking with the subject for a few minutes, the subject dropped the weapon, which turned out to be a fork instead of a knife, and subject was turned over to mental health.

One night, while working the night watch dispatching, a car pulled up into the police parking lot, and a young female got out, and at this time we had a buzzer and intercom system, and after speaking with the subject on the intercom, I buzzed her in, and when she came into the office she advised she had been at a bar with her boyfriend. I took all her information and her boyfriend's name, and she advised he was very violent and had hit her and reached into the vehicle while she was leaving the bar and broke off her key in the vehicle while it was running. And she just came to the police station and wanted to file a report and have him arrested and that he beat her up all the time. I dispatched the officer to the station and explained to him what we had. The officer came in and took the complaint from the alleged victim, and about two weeks later, I was speaking with the assistant prosecutor, who advised he might have me come in to testify about the incident where the female came in to the police office because she was dropping all the charges. I advised him I would be glad to do so if he thought we could win the case, and I never heard anything more, so I guess they dropped the charges.

We had one incident where two officers were dispatched to a domestic, and the officers arrived at the scene and had to fight with the complainant's husband, a very large drunk man, and they had arrested and took the subject to jail. And before morning, the suspect's wife, the victim, was trying to bail her wife-battering husband out of jail, and all the officers frowned on those type of incidents after risking their lives to help.

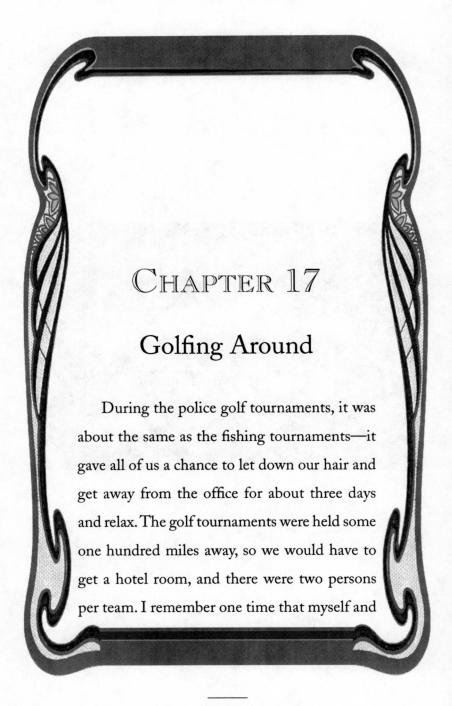

CHAPTER 17

Golfing Around

During the police golf tournaments, it was about the same as the fishing tournaments—it gave all of us a chance to let down our hair and get away from the office for about three days and relax. The golf tournaments were held some one hundred miles away, so we would have to get a hotel room, and there were two persons per team. I remember one time that myself and another officer was scheduled to play in the police golf tournament, and he advised me the day we were to leave that he was not going to be able to play, so I went down with another officer friend and his buddy who were to play in the tournament. Upon arrival at the hotel where we would be staying, I found they had no extra rooms available, so the officer I came with advised me I could move a rollaway bed into their room, so that's what I did. And since I did not have a partner, I was advised to hit two times in the two-man best-ball tournament. That sounded good, but it really wears you out since I was just average, but that's what I did and still had a great time.

Some of the guys at the hotel room played cards and drank and relaxed. The next day, I remember one officer who was playing golf with his son who was in our foursome, four persons per tee, so the officer and his son golfed alongside of us. He looked to be in his forties, and his son around eighteen to twenty, and while playing one of the holes, the officer advised us he was having a battle with cancer and this was the first time he and his son had a chance to do anything for some time since he was in treatment. You couldn't tell it; they both smoked us, and you could tell they really had a great relationship. The sad part about it was that about two months later, I heard that the officer had expired. I would also like to add that when you have one hundred police officers out on the links at one time, you hear an echo of fours, and I thought that was funny.

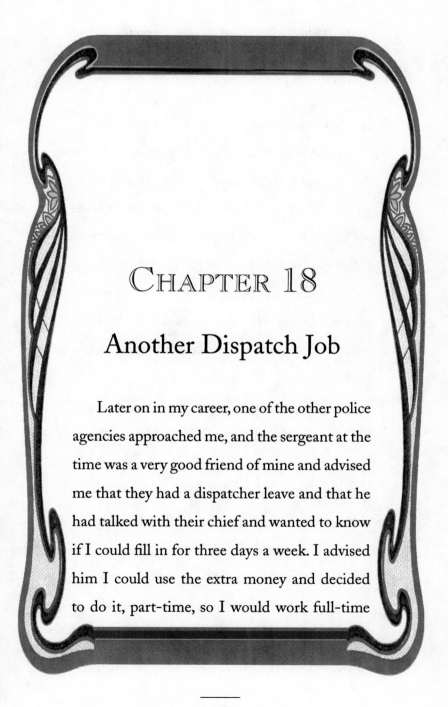

CHAPTER 18

Another Dispatch Job

Later on in my career, one of the other police agencies approached me, and the sergeant at the time was a very good friend of mine and advised me that they had a dispatcher leave and that he had talked with their chief and wanted to know if I could fill in for three days a week. I advised him I could use the extra money and decided to do it, part-time, so I would work full-time for one agency and work three days a week for another agency as a jailer and dispatcher.

I had to make sure the prisoners were dressed out in their orange jumpsuits, and there was an officer there with me most of the time, and they had a cell block and four different smaller cells, which had four bunk beds and a toilet and a barred door for each cell. I would advise prisoners that they could go out into the cell block as long as they were not causing any problems, and the prisoners would get three meals a day, and on my shift that consisted of a TV dinner with their choice of either water of coffee. I would take the food to the drop-down door at the main cell block; most of the time this was just a holding cell, and they bonded out after a couple of days.

Another time the fire department was called to a vehicle on fire, and when the officer arrived at the scene, the emergency squad came and took the owner and another subject to the hospital, and after observation and testing was conducted on the two, the officer went to the hospital to get a statement from the subjects. And when the officer asked the owner what caused their vehicle to blow up, the owner advised the officer that while at the gas station, he opened his gas lid on his vehicle and used his lighter to see if there was any fuel in the vehicle, and it blew up in their face. Needless to say, both subjects were okay.

CHAPTER 19

Hazard County

I remember in another county they had a sheriff and one deputy and a town cop in the county seat, and they rolled in the sidewalks after dark in this sleepy little town and never had a lot of crime nor had much going on, almost like Mayberry. And they never had a police dispatch or communications department, and in those

Joseph L. Swick

days 911 was just three numbers, and all police communications went through our radio.

One day, the only police officer that was in the town retired, and the town was looking for someone else to take his place. And they found their man, a younger guy, very eager. His name was Officer Epsilon; he came into the department as police chief and the only officer in the area. While I was working the night watch in Dispatch, it seemed like every night or so, Officer Epsilon would call in a pursuit. Everything would be quiet when I would hear him exclaim on the radio, "I'm in pursuit! I'm in pursuit!" in a high pitched voice, only to say later, "I lost them," and call off the pursuit.

One night, I remember that after he was there for about three weeks, Officer Epsilon called in a pursuit and advised a brief description of the vehicle and location, and he advised in a

122

high pitched voice, "And I'm being shot at from the pursued vehicle." And again he advised he lost contact with vehicle a few seconds later and called off the pursuit.

Another time on a Friday night, Officer Epsilon was again in pursuit, this time of a vehicle from a neighboring state, for running a stop sign, and the suspect ran off the road at a high rate of speed, and the suspect was killed. All of this in just six weeks on the job. A few days later the police garage where Officer Epsilon's cruiser was kept caught fire and was put out without incident, and a few days later, Officer Epsilon was looking for another job. In just two months, this officer had been involved in more incidents than most officers have in a thirty-year career.

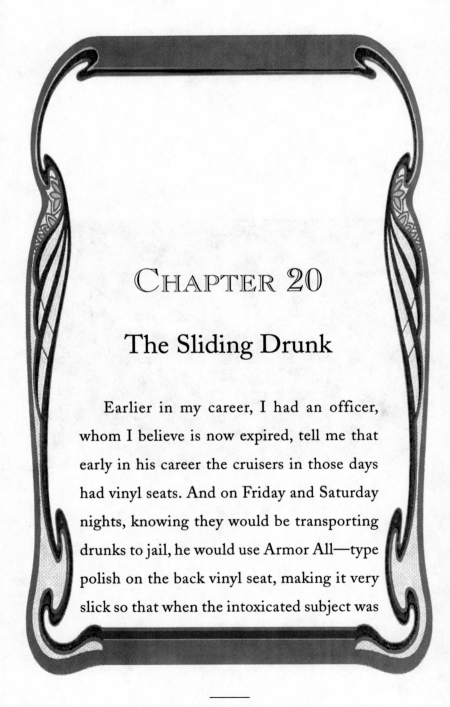

Chapter 20

The Sliding Drunk

Earlier in my career, I had an officer, whom I believe is now expired, tell me that early in his career the cruisers in those days had vinyl seats. And on Friday and Saturday nights, knowing they would be transporting drunks to jail, he would use Armor All—type polish on the back vinyl seat, making it very slick so that when the intoxicated subject was put into the cruiser, he would bounce side to side in the cruiser like a ping pong ball while taking the curves in the road at high speed. In those days I guess laws were different. Of course years later, when I retired from the department, if anyone was caught doing something like that, he most likely would be fired and/or sued.

And also in the early days, the local hospitals worked with the police departments, and they had a great relationship, so if an officer would have to fight with some drunk and use force and afterward bring in an intoxicated man to the hospital to get sutured or other treatment, if the subject was being obnoxious or rude to the personnel, it's been said that the doctor may sew up a head wound without anesthetic, or a nurse may put in a catheter when one was not needed. So in those days, if you were brought

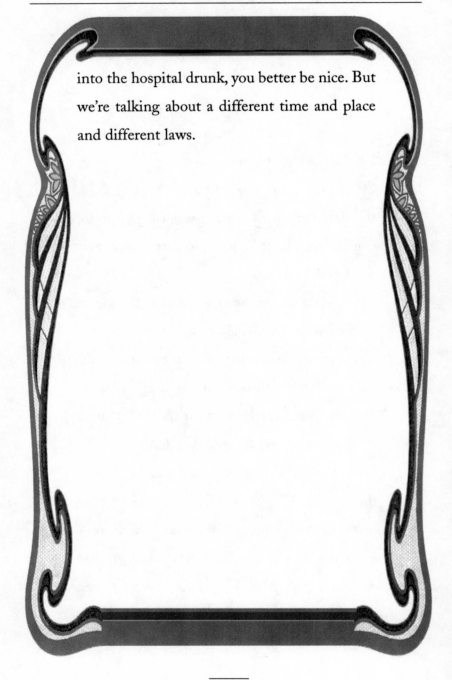

into the hospital drunk, you better be nice. But we're talking about a different time and place and different laws.

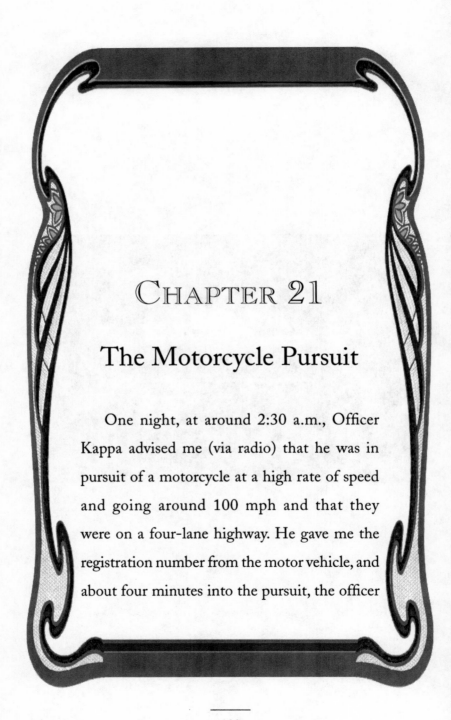

CHAPTER 21

The Motorcycle Pursuit

One night, at around 2:30 a.m., Officer Kappa advised me (via radio) that he was in pursuit of a motorcycle at a high rate of speed and going around 100 mph and that they were on a four-lane highway. He gave me the registration number from the motor vehicle, and about four minutes into the pursuit, the officer advised, "Call the emergency squad, the suspect just left the road."

I called the emergency squad and a tow truck as well, thinking this subject just left the highway on a bike and was most likely dead. And in about five minutes, the officer advised me on the radio that he could not find the suspect after searching the area where his bike had just hit a tree going 100 mph.

So no one was found, but later the officer came into the office carrying the bent-up handle bars and some other parts from the wrecked motorcycle and explained, "This is what's left of the motorcycle that had hit a tree going 100 mph." And of course later that morning, the motorcycle was called in and reported stolen. The officer told me later that he went to the residence of the owner of the motorcycle and found there was a man lying on the couch, partly covered up and looked to be in pain, but the subjects there advised he just had the flu and was asleep. The officer advised he was sure that was the guy who had been on the bike the night before and staggered home drunk, but he couldn't prove it, and if the man had not been drunk, he would most likely be dead.

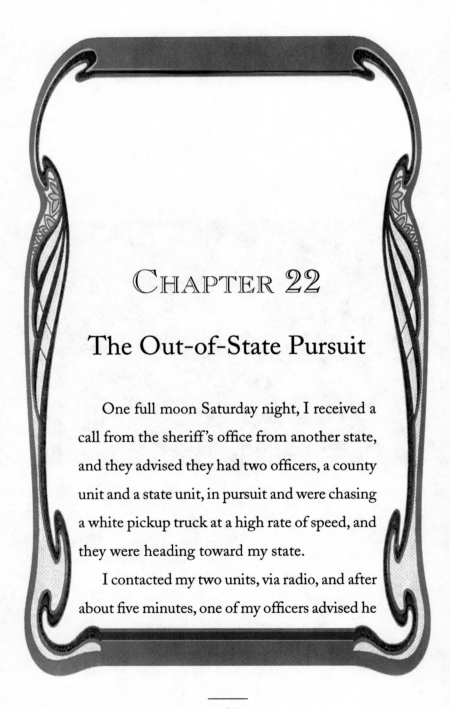

Chapter 22

The Out-of-State Pursuit

One full moon Saturday night, I received a
call from the sheriff's office from another state,
and they advised they had two officers, a county
unit and a state unit, in pursuit and were chasing
a white pickup truck at a high rate of speed, and
they were heading toward my state.

I contacted my two units, via radio, and after
about five minutes, one of my officers advised he

had a visual on the suspect, but he was headed toward them and subject just passed him with the out-of-state officers on his tail. The other officer that we had out overheard the radio traffic and was up ahead, and he advised me he would be setting up a vehicle-rolling roadblock with his cruiser in the middle of the roadway.

Next I heard the officer say, "I see the subject coming," and when the suspect saw his cruiser in the middle of the road with all lights on, he ran off the road and hit a tree, and the officer advised me to call the emergency squad and towing. And I did, and later the officer advised that when he went up to the wrecked vehicle, he found that both males in the vehicle were expired and that the driver had a automatic handgun with the seat belt wrapped around his hand. The gun was loaded and off safety, and the subject was ready to shoot whoever pulled him over; if he had not wrecked his vehicle, they most likely would have shot someone.

Another time, at around 6:00 a.m. on a Sunday morning, I received a call from an old farmer who advised he had picked up some dynamite that he had stored for some time in an old outbuilding for blowing up stumps and had it in his pickup truck, and that it was leaking some type of substance all over his truck bed. I advised him not to let anyone touch or go near the truck because it was most likely broken down into nitroglycerin, and he was lucky he never blew up anything. I notified Officer Lamba, who came out, and the explosives were contained, and it ended without incident.

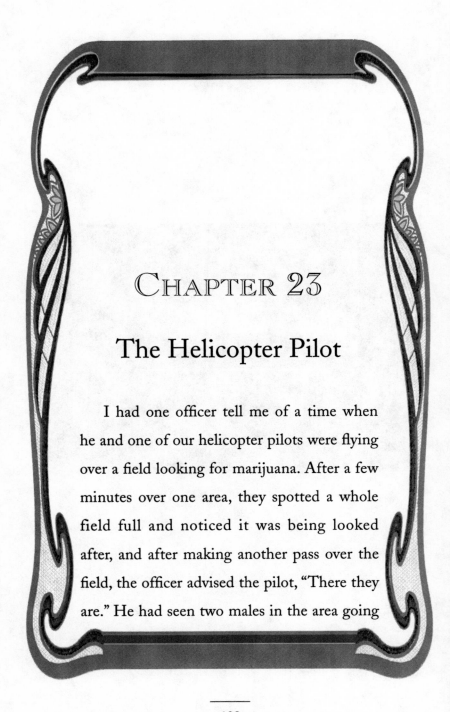

CHAPTER 23

The Helicopter Pilot

I had one officer tell me of a time when he and one of our helicopter pilots were flying over a field looking for marijuana. After a few minutes over one area, they spotted a whole field full and noticed it was being looked after, and after making another pass over the field, the officer advised the pilot, "There they are." He had seen two males in the area going toward their vehicle, and the ex-military pilot set the craft down in the middle of the field, and the large prop was touching leaves of trees on each side of the field, and the subjects were apprehended and charged. But the officer, who most of the time was very calm, advised me that when the pilot put the helicopter down, he did get very excited.

Also, another time, the same helicopter pilot and the same officer were out during a major flood in our area, and they saw a subject hanging on to a rock in the river. The pilot advised the officer that he thought he could put one of the rudders from the helicopter on a big rock in the river and hover over while the officer pulled the subject from the high water, and the pilot proceeded, and a life was saved. The officer would later say, "That helicopter pilot is the bravest man I've ever known." The helicopter pilot had found several lost hunters and lost fishermen, and when I left the department, the helicopter pilot was still flying.

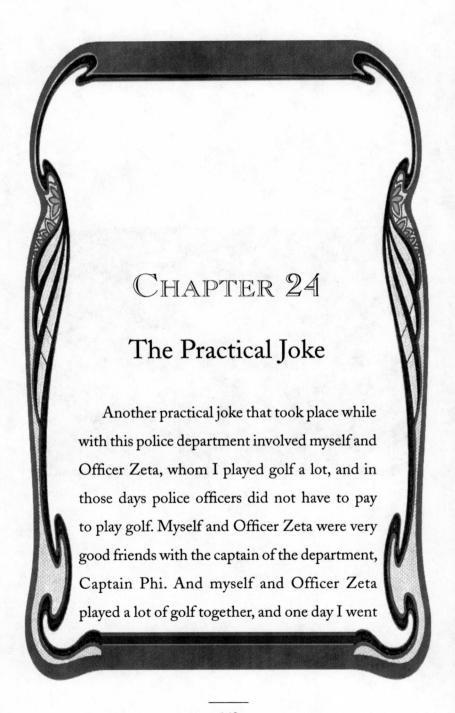

CHAPTER 24

The Practical Joke

Another practical joke that took place while with this police department involved myself and Officer Zeta, whom I played golf a lot, and in those days police officers did not have to pay to play golf. Myself and Officer Zeta were very good friends with the captain of the department, Captain Phi. And myself and Officer Zeta played a lot of golf together, and one day I went to Officer Zeta's residence, and we were to play golf in another county, and when I showed up, I was wearing white knickers and wearing one of those funny-looking hats sitting sideways on my head. Officer Zeta advised he wanted to take a picture of me in my knickers, so I held out a golf club, and Officer Zeta took the photo. And we proceeded with our outing and had a great day on the links.

I really never thought much about the photo that Officer Zeta had taken, until I was called into the captain's office a few weeks later, and he showed me a copy of the monthly police newsletter and turned to the page that showed articles of incidents that had happened in our department, and in that location of the paper was a picture of me in my knickers and a story at the bottom. It stated,

Dapper Joe, Mr. Swick, our dispatcher, when not working loves to go out on the links and play golf, but he has one handicap; his handicap is playing golf with Captain Pi.

And pretending not to have known about the article, he asked, "What the hell is this? Don't you like playing golf with me, and why did you put this in the paper?" And I advised him I did not put that in the paper, and I blamed it on First Sergeant Alpha, who was standing there laughing at the time and denied it. We later had a good laugh over that joke, and that's the way things were in those days. If you were liked, the officers played jokes on you; if not, they would stay away from you.

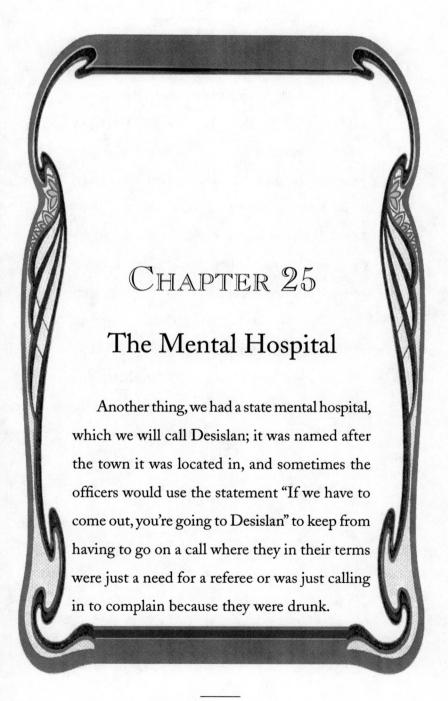

CHAPTER 25

The Mental Hospital

Another thing, we had a state mental hospital, which we will call Desislan; it was named after the town it was located in, and sometimes the officers would use the statement "If we have to come out, you're going to Desislan" to keep from having to go on a call where they in their terms were just a need for a referee or was just calling in to complain because they were drunk.

Most of the subjects who were taken there, at some time in their lifetime, to Desislan (mental hospital) must have had some bad, bad memories because when an officer would say, "If we have to come out, you're going to jail," they didn't blink an eye, but if they said, "You're going to Desislan," they would sober up in a split second and would advise the officer that everything was fine now and they didn't need an officer. So Desislan must have been a real hell.

One night, on a weekend night, Mrs. X, a regular caller, was drunk and called in, cussing and yelling, and advised her boyfriend had taken her cigarettes and wouldn't give them to her, and she had knocked him down the steps at the residence. Mrs. X was a big, burly lady, and every time she got drunk, she would beat up her boyfriend. And Mrs. X had been taken to Desislan before.

So Officer Delta was advised on station, and Officer Delta spoke with the subject on the phone and advised her that if he had to come out there, her boyfriend was going to jail and she would be taken to Desislan, and the officer hung up the phone. In about one minute, the phone rings, and Mrs. X is on the phone. She advised, "Do not send out an officer here, I now have my cigarettes and we're getting along fine." So I guess for those days the fear of Desislan worked.

One night at around 3:00 a.m., I received a call from a subject advising of a vehicle that had wrecked and was on its top. No one was hurt, but there was one young man standing around the vehicle; it happened about three miles west of the office. I dispatched Officer Delta, and upon arrival, he called for a tow truck, which I dispatched, and then ran a DMV check on the registration.

About fifteen minutes later, Officer Delta brought the driver of the vehicle back to the office, and he looked to be around eighteen years old, and the officer advised him to sit in the lobby and not to move, and Officer Delta came into the radio room and had me run the subject's license, which came back okay. And then Officer Delta advised me, after talking with the subject, to call the subject's mother and have her come in and pick up her son. I made the call, and his mother advised she would be at the office in a few minutes to pick up her son.

Meanwhile, I heard the officer advise the subject, who was walking toward the door, to sit down. The subject cussed the officer and said he didn't have to sit down. Next the officer had the subject in handcuffs and advised me to call the magistrate on call to come out because now the subject was under arrest; the subject had been drinking some, and the officer tried to cut the young man a break, and he was too out of it or on too much of an ego trip to see it.

Officer Delta advised he would be transporting the subject to jail and asked me to advise his mother when she came in as to what had happen. Later his mother showed up, and I advised her of everything that had happened, that she would have to contact the jail to see her son now, and that the officer gave him several chances to comply and he would not be arrested and he refused.

I had another officer, Officer Nu, advise of a story a long time ago when he had first started. He advised that his training officer, who had started in the late 1960s, told him a story when he first started. He was in pursuit one night and

Joseph L. Swick

was following the vehicle out of town at a high rate of speed, and after about ten minutes into the pursuit, the officer put down the driver-side window on his cruiser and held his .38 police revolver out of the window and began shooting at the tires of the fleeing vehicle. One bullet hit the tire of the vehicle and the vehicle was stopped and the subject was arrested. In those days that was the norm.

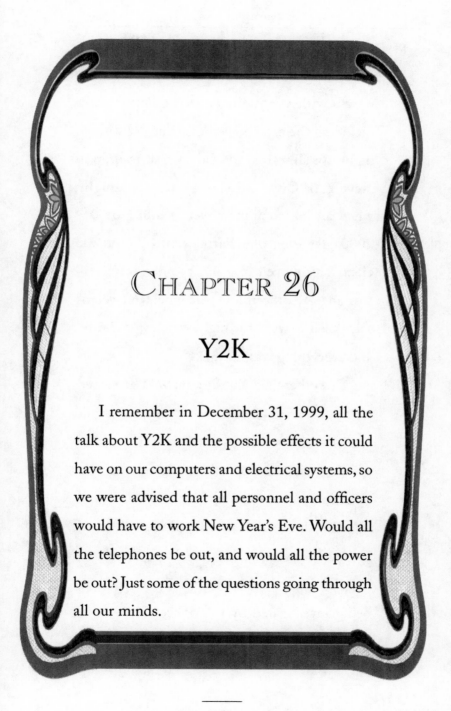

CHAPTER 26

Y2K

I remember in December 31, 1999, all the talk about Y2K and the possible effects it could have on our computers and electrical systems, so we were advised that all personnel and officers would have to work New Year's Eve. Would all the telephones be out, and would all the power be out? Just some of the questions going through all our minds.

So with every officer in the department, including the captain, working that New Year's night, we all waited for the big ball to drop in New York City, and shortly after midnight, when all the computers were reading 01-01-2000, not even one alarm went off, and the electricity stayed on, and phones were still working. All officers and personnel who weren't scheduled to work the night watch went home, and everything was normal.

One other time, shortly after 9/11 happened, we received several calls where someone would receive white powder in the mail or find a white powdery substance on a floor in a restroom, but none turned out to be anthrax.

Also, during the same day of the 9/11 attack in New York and Washington, D.C., there was a large jet spotted over the local airport, and after being investigated by the police and after all

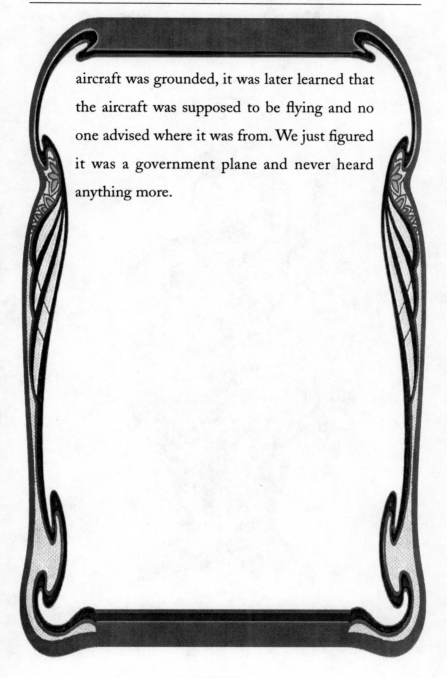

aircraft was grounded, it was later learned that the aircraft was supposed to be flying and no one advised where it was from. We just figured it was a government plane and never heard anything more.

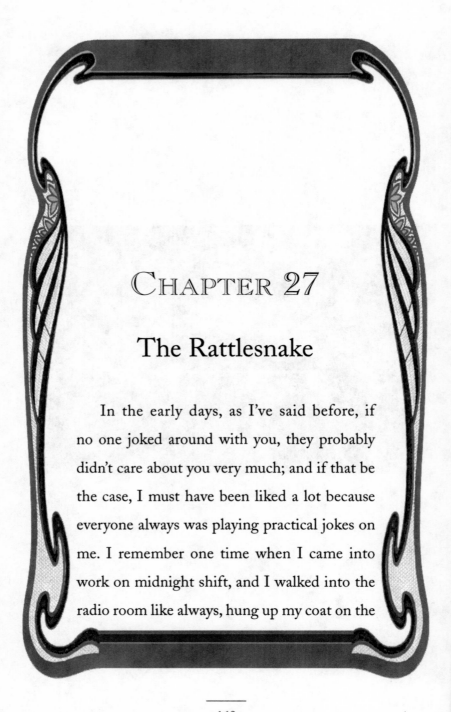

CHAPTER 27

The Rattlesnake

In the early days, as I've said before, if no one joked around with you, they probably didn't care about you very much; and if that be the case, I must have been liked a lot because everyone always was playing practical jokes on me. I remember one time when I came into work on midnight shift, and I walked into the radio room like always, hung up my coat on the hook, and went downstairs to make coffee, and came back up the steps into the radio room to check my mailbox, which was one of the shelves on the wall.

This one time, I noticed there were three officers in the radio room and the evening dispatcher. When I looked into my mailbox, there was a very large rattlesnake looking at me, and all I saw was fangs. It had been ran over by a vehicle on the highway, and one of the officers there was going to make something out of it; they had put it there to scare me, and it worked, and whatever reaction they expected, they got more! I jumped and shivered and got the hell out of there as fast as I could move until I found it was dead, and they had put a pen in its mouth to show its fangs. Afterward, we all had a good laugh.

Another prank that one of the dispatchers would pull was with the computer paper, and at that time, the computer paper had holes that had to be lined up, and when it ran out, you had to go through a lot of steps to load it and line up the holes. One of the other dispatchers, before his shift would end, would go down about three pages and tear off the paper, and put it back on top of the other paper, and about one hour into my shift, I would run something for an officer, and most of the time on one the busy nights, the paper looked as if it had ran out of paper, and I would have to reroute the paper which, would slow down my work progress; needless to say I returned the favor and put a stop to that.

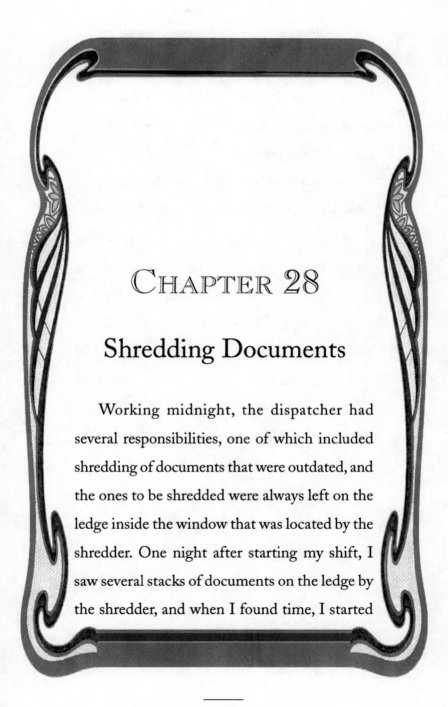

Chapter 28

Shredding Documents

Working midnight, the dispatcher had several responsibilities, one of which included shredding of documents that were outdated, and the ones to be shredded were always left on the ledge inside the window that was located by the shredder. One night after starting my shift, I saw several stacks of documents on the ledge by the shredder, and when I found time, I started shredding until all was shredded, and the next morning I went home and was sleeping when the telephone rang.

It was the chief dispatcher; she wanted to know where the documents were that the evening dispatcher left on the window ledge. Knowing that nothing could be saved on the computer at the time, I advised, "I thought they were to be shredded, and I shredded them all." I heard silence, and she advised, "Those were not to be shredded," and I advised her that all documents left on the window ledge by the shredder was always shredded. After seeing it was not all my fault, she called the main office, who sent all important documents to her office.

Another story was relayed to me by another dispatcher in another area. He had dispatched two officers to a bar fight, and one of the officers was a K-9 officer. Upon arrival, they found that a man had been hit with a broken beer bottle and had his ear cut off. After breaking up the fight and calling the emergency squad, they started looking for the man's ear. After looking for a while, the K-9 officer looked down at his German shepherd, who was seen with his nose under a table; and when the officer pulled his chain, he noticed the dog was licking his chops. It's believed that the dog had made a snack out of the man's cut-off ear because they never did find it.

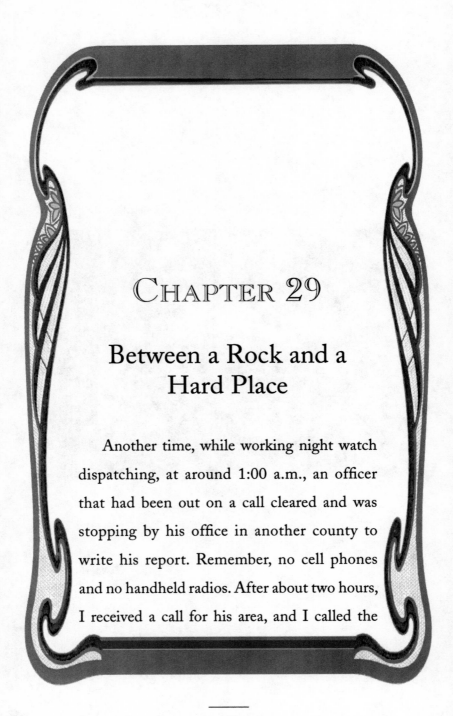

CHAPTER 29

Between a Rock and a Hard Place

Another time, while working night watch dispatching, at around 1:00 a.m., an officer that had been out on a call cleared and was stopping by his office in another county to write his report. Remember, no cell phones and no handheld radios. After about two hours, I received a call for his area, and I called the number at the office, and there was no answer. I tried his car radio, and after a few minutes, I called the backup unit on call, advised him that the other officer had been out of his cruiser at his office for approximately two hours and there was no answer when I called the office and there was no radio contact on his car radio.

So the other officer went to check on him, and after getting out of his vehicle at the office, he called me on the office phone and advised that he had found the officer between the entry door and the main door, which would lock automatically behind whoever walked in. The officer in question had forgotten his keys and was stuck and locked between the doors and was okay; he was just waiting for someone to come to the office. After that, the officer never forgot his keys again.

Another time we had several officers out where a coal mine had an explosion and entrapped thirteen miners, and after the police and fire department had set up a mobile command and communications post, and after days of trying to get to the miners, the workers got to the entrapped men. Somehow, with bad radio reception to the command post from the workers, the police and media were advised that twelve of the men had survived, and one had expired. After watching the local and national news reporting that the twelve survivors were being brought out, I received a call from one of our officers in another county who advised that he and two other officers from their area were going to the mine because the communications were wrong and twelve miners had expired and only one survived, and they expected trouble when they heard the truth.

Chapter 30

The Rifle Man

One night, I received a call from a male subject who advised that his vehicle had been shot at from someone on the road bank hidden in the weeds, and I dispatched the officer on call, and nothing was found.

A few days later, I was working the night watch, and around 2:00 a.m., I received another call from another trucker who advised he was being shot at in the same area and was calling from someone's residence near the shooting. He advised that he saw a white sports car driving up and down the area and believed they were possible suspects.

I advised the officer on call, and this time two officers went to the scene. And they pulled over the white sports car and found two males and a loaded .22 rifle in the vehicle, and suspects were arrested, and that ended the shootings.

One other time, we were investigating an incident where a subject in a car was chasing a truck driver, and the truck driver pulled over, and the subject in the car shot the truck driver, and the truck driver was taken to the hospital.

When I came on that night, I was advised of the incident and never thought any more about it until around 5:00 a.m., when I received a call from one of our local TV stations. The lady asked if we were working a case where a truck driver was shot. I advised her I have no information for the media on any shooting; she then advised me that she had heard that the truck driver had expired. I advised her I did not hear any information from the hospital on anyone or anything, and she hung up.

At around 6:00 a.m., I was watching the TV station and saw the person I had just spoken with earlier, and my throat got a lump in it when I heard her say, "Mr. Swick, the police dispatcher, confirmed there was a shooting of a truck driver in their area." That couldn't have been farther from the truth, and I could have gotten into trouble for that media mistake. And it was a long time before that TV station ever got much more than a good-bye from me.

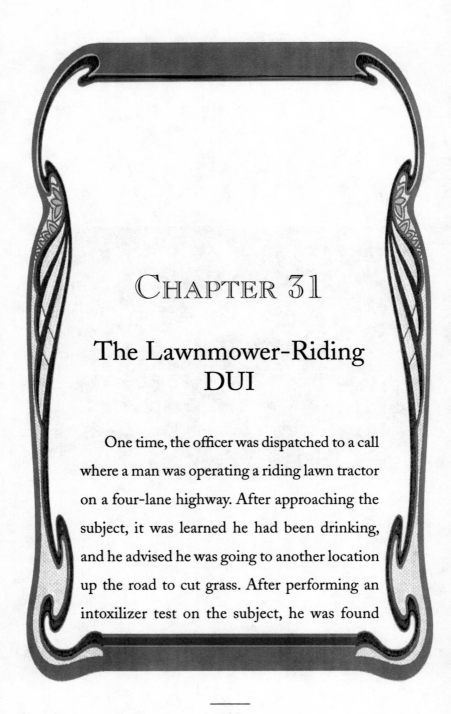

Chapter 31

The Lawnmower-Riding DUI

One time, the officer was dispatched to a call where a man was operating a riding lawn tractor on a four-lane highway. After approaching the subject, it was learned he had been drinking, and he advised he was going to another location up the road to cut grass. After performing an intoxilizer test on the subject, he was found to have been intoxicated and was arrested for DUI.

Another story was about two cousins, both young females, who grew up in one of the counties in our area. They were always in some sort of trouble. Ever since the time they were old enough to drive, there was always some type of problem; and when they were old enough to go to a bar, they were involved in a fight, it seemed like, every week.

Both females were very attractive, and even when they were in college, we got complaints from the subjects when they came home, most of the time some type of domestic or bar fights. It was believed that the subjects were from a well-to-do family, and I think they moved out of state after college to another town, and if there is a party going on there, I'm sure both will be there.

Another story that came from a coworker whom I worked with, and he advised one evening while dispatching that a young lady came into the office wearing a see-through nightgown and yelling, and she advised that her boyfriend was outside in their vehicle and needed a handcuff key to unlock his handcuffs. The dispatcher advised the officer on call, and the officer asked the young female, "Why is your boyfriend handcuffed?" And she advised him that they were playing around and lost the key, so the officer went out to the parking lot to unlock the handcuffs and found a male subject who rose up from the back of their pickup truck holding up a headboard from their bed, which the subject was still handcuffed to. The officer unlocked the handcuffs and both subjects left.

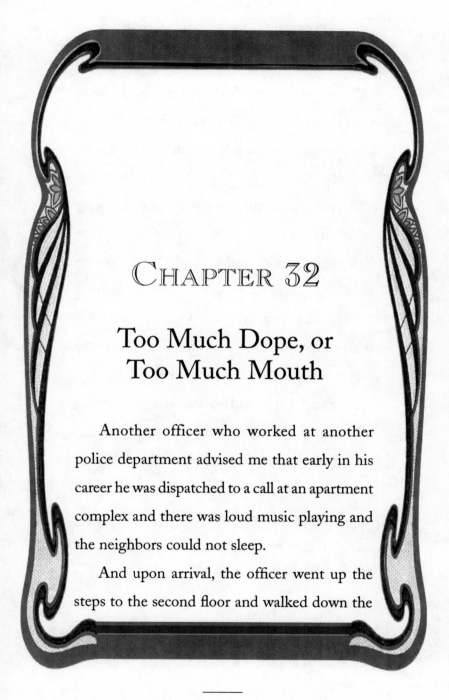

CHAPTER 32

Too Much Dope, or Too Much Mouth

Another officer who worked at another police department advised me that early in his career he was dispatched to a call at an apartment complex and there was loud music playing and the neighbors could not sleep.

And upon arrival, the officer went up the steps to the second floor and walked down the hallway toward the apartment where the loud music was banging. The officer knocked on the apartment door and advised, "This is the police!"

A twentysomething male subject with long brown hair tied in a ponytail came to the door. Before the officer could explain to the young man that he needed to turn down his loud music, the young man—looking at the officer with glassy, wild eyes—told the officer, "I know why you're here. Okay, you got me."

He said that he had been smoking marijuana. The officer was about to say, "I need to search your apartment," when the subject said, "I'll go get it."

After about two minutes, the subject came back and, with the door still opened, gave the officer a plastic bag that contained what appeared to be marijuana and two joints, all before the officer could advise the subject he was under arrest!

The subject explained, "Wait, I've got more!" and went into another room.

The officer heard doors and drawers opening and closing. The young man came back with pipes, a bong, even more dope, and paraphernalia.

Just like that, without looking for anything or being there other than to advise the subject to turn down his loud music, the officer ended up making a felony arrest. If the young man would have kept his mouth closed and just waited for the officer to tell him why he was there, there would not have been any reason for the officer to arrest the subject.

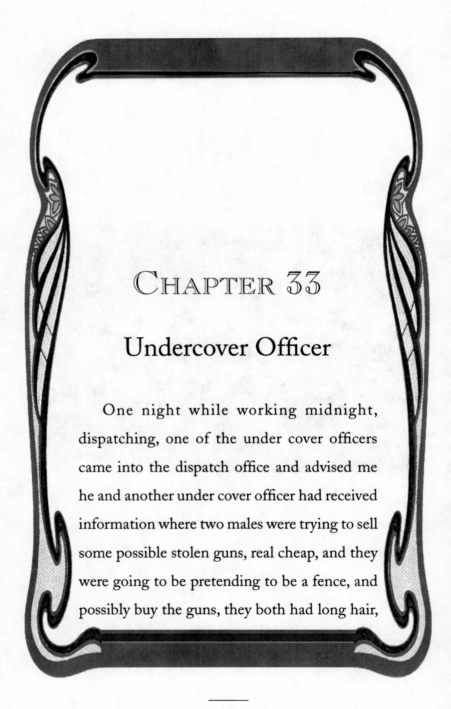

Chapter 33

Undercover Officer

One night while working midnight, dispatching, one of the under cover officers came into the dispatch office and advised me he and another under cover officer had received information where two males were trying to sell some possible stolen guns, real cheap, and they were going to be pretending to be a fence, and possibly buy the guns, they both had long hair, and were wearing dirty jeans, and had facial scruff, and they went to the duplex apartment up stairs and went in to the residence, and two males had twelve guns laying on the bed, and wanted $2000.00 for them, everything from new rifles to new shot guns, while the two officers were pretending to look over the guns, they had a note pad conceled and was writing down serial numbers from the guns, and advised the subjects they did not have any money on them but had to go to there residence and get it and bring it back , and left telling the subjects they would be back in about twenty minutes.

And the officers then brought the serial numbers back onstation and into the dispatch room for me to run on the computer to see if any or all were stolen, and I did, and all came back stolen, and then the officers contacted two uniformed officers from are department and notified the sergeant in another department they were going back to the duplex, and pretend to buy the guns, and so the officers don't get his cover blown, they would have to be arrested with the subjects with the guns on some type of fake warant from another neighboring state, and after the officers was in the duplex for about 5 minutes the Sargent and a young new officer knocked on the door with the fake warrant for the under cover officers, and when the officers came in one of the male subject jumped out of the two story window, and awaiting them was two police officers from are department who apprehended the subject, and mean while in the apartment the other subject was arresed, also the under cover officers, and one of the new police officers who was unaware that the other subject was an under cover police officer, when back onstation the sergeant instructed the younger new officer who had arrrested one of the under cover officers and found a gun in his boot and was being a little rough with him, you can take off the hand cuffs now he is an under cover state officer, the younger officer turned three different shades, and was stunned.

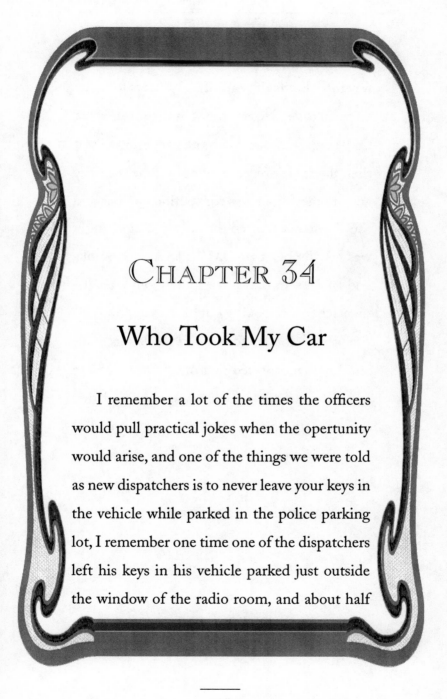

CHAPTER 34

Who Took My Car

I remember a lot of the times the officers would pull practical jokes when the opertunity would arise, and one of the things we were told as new dispatchers is to never leave your keys in the vehicle while parked in the police parking lot, I remember one time one of the dispatchers left his keys in his vehicle parked just outside the window of the radio room, and about half way into there shift, one of the officers took the dispachers vehicle and put it in the wash bay in the garage and put down the garage door, and then the same officer went out on the highway and ran the dispatchers registration number, and the dispatcher advised the officer after seeing it was his number, that DMV advised not on file, and later on in the shift about a hour later the dispatcher was looking out of the window onto the parking lot and found his vehicle was gone, and he then contaced that officer who had ran his plate that his vehicle was gone , and that had been the plate the officer had ran earlier, and after leting the dispatcher stew for awhile , the officer advised the dispatcher that they had moved his vehicle into the wash bay.

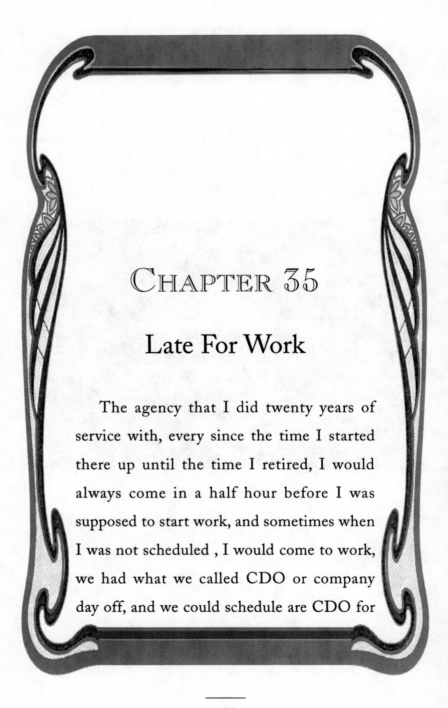

CHAPTER 35

Late For Work

The agency that I did twenty years of service with, every since the time I started there up until the time I retired, I would always come in a half hour before I was supposed to start work, and sometimes when I was not scheduled , I would come to work, we had what we called CDO or company day off, and we could schedule are CDO for the month, but I advised my chief dispatcher to just schedule mine with my days off and so I never scheduled my C D Os. So a lot of the time I would forget we had a C D O for that month and would come into work , and on those nights just as if the officers and dispatcher who were working that night knew that I would be coming into work not knowing I had a C D O, they would grab my lunch as I walked in the door, and I knew something was up, and found out I was not supposed to be there and would go home, but one night when I came in, no one let on , the other dispatcher knowing I was not supposed to be there left as soon as I came in, and I started my paper work , signed on, and started reading the prior shifts logs, and about a half hour later, I notice one of the other dispatchers coming into the driveway, and then it hit me, I'm not supposed to be here, and when the other dispatcher came in I explained , I now know I'm not supposed to be here, and then I went home. I always figured I would rather show up when I'm not supposed to be at work, than not to show up when I'm scheduled.

Another time I got revenge on the other dispatcher, indirectly, I had scheduled a vacation that I thought was for two weeks, and on paper I had put in for only one week, and the end of the first week my girlfriend and I went to the beach about 4 hundred miles away, and on the last night at the hotel at around 12 am, I received a call from the police department, it was the same dispatcher whom had left early on the night he knew I was not supposed to be there,,,,he advised why arent you at work, I advised I'm at the beach and on vacation, and he explained , no you only put in for one week and you are do back tonight,

I advised him that I had made a mistake and to put me off and I will be back to work tomorrow night . . . . so fate caught up with that other dispatcher . . . .

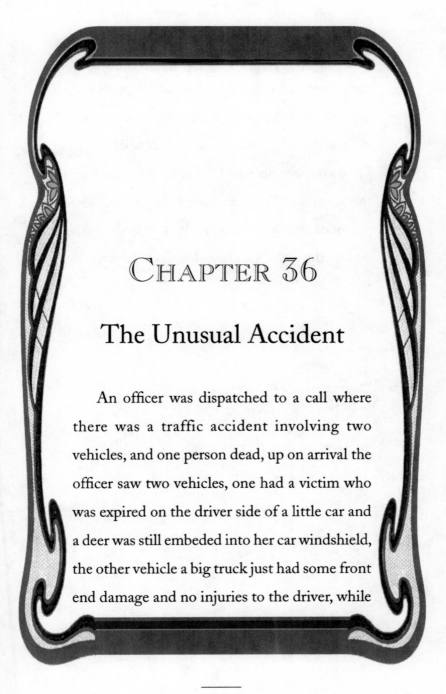

Chapter 36

The Unusual Accident

An officer was dispatched to a call where there was a traffic accident involving two vehicles, and one person dead, up on arrival the officer saw two vehicles, one had a victim who was expired on the driver side of a little car and a deer was still embedded into her car windshield, the other vehicle a big truck just had some front end damage and no injuries to the driver, while the officer was conducting his investigation he learned from the other driver who was driving his truck south bound at a high rate of speed , had struck a deer and sending the deer into the air and at the oncoming car, and the deer proceded through the other drivers windshield, and in the freak accident the truck driver was not charged.

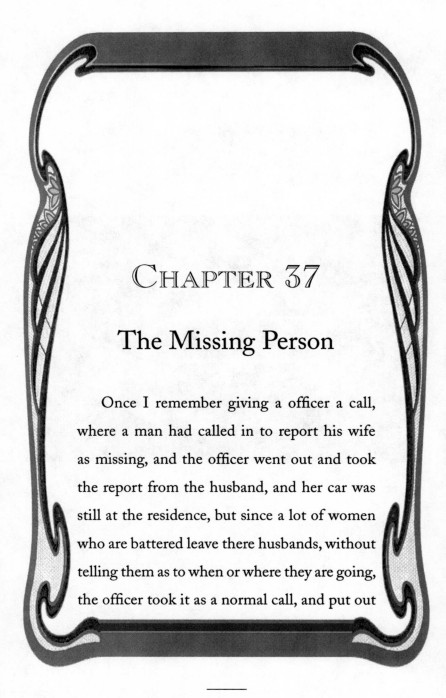

CHAPTER 37

The Missing Person

Once I remember giving a officer a call, where a man had called in to report his wife as missing, and the officer went out and took the report from the husband, and her car was still at the residence, but since a lot of women who are battered leave there husbands, without telling them as to when or where they are going, the officer took it as a normal call, and put out a BOLO be on the look out, and as the week went on the husband started calling in more and more and wanting to know if we have found his missing wife, we advised no and after about three days the ladies family started calling the officer and wanting to know where there relative was, and this time two officers went back out to the husbands residence and now faul play was being suspected, but after a breif search of the ladies car, the house and around the house, she was not to be found. And on the fourth day the husband called back in again and wanted to know if we had any information as to where his wife was, I advised no and that he would be one of the first contacted if we find her, and he hung up, and later that week he called back again and explained he had accidently killed her and that her body is in the back yard under some rubish, and the officers went to the residnece and found

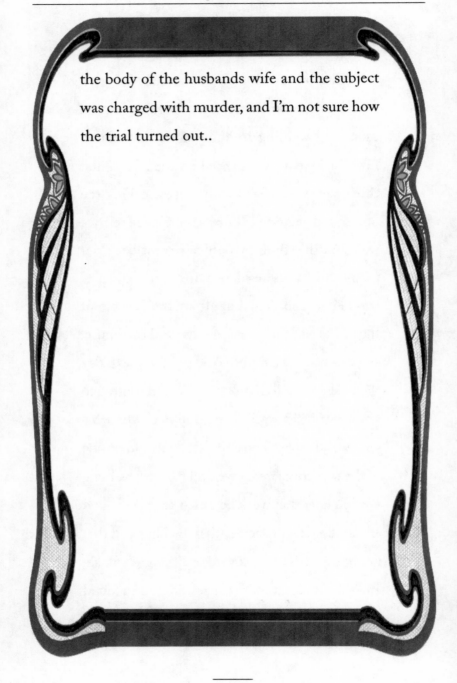

the body of the husbands wife and the subject

was charged with murder, and I'm not sure how

the trial turned out..

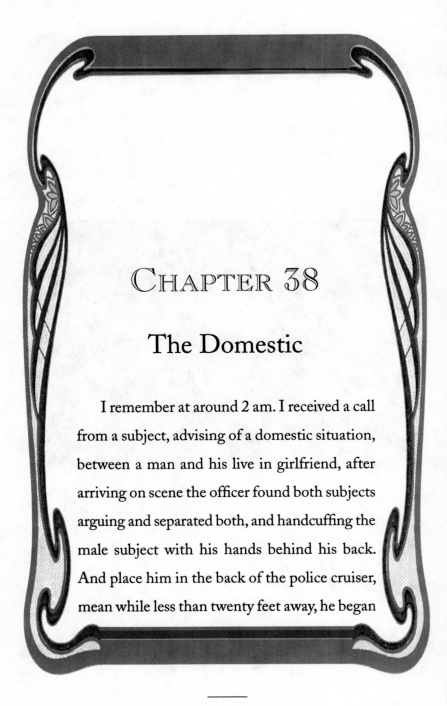

CHAPTER 38

The Domestic

I remember at around 2 am. I received a call from a subject, advising of a domestic situation, between a man and his live in girlfriend, after arriving on scene the officer found both subjects arguing and separated both, and handcuffing the male subject with his hands behind his back. And place him in the back of the police cruiser, mean while less than twenty feet away, he began taking a statement from the female, and would take a statement from the male afterwords, and since they were just arguing, the male subject would have to be taken to another residence away from the female.

After the officer who was still about twenty feet from his cruiser was finishing up taking the statement from the female, when the officer noticed the male subject whom he had placed in the back of his cruiser, now had his handcuffs, in front of him and had also obtained the shotgun that the officer had in his front seat, and the male subject placed the shotgun to his head before the officer could get to the cruiser the man had shot himself in the head , knocking out the whole back glass of the said cruiser, the officer had me dispatch E M S, and I did, and also the officer proformed C P R. on the subject and did everything he could to stop the blood.

If the man had not took his own life, the officer most likely would have just escorted the young man home, another thing in those days, the police cruisers was not conformed to carey a shotgun and they had no gunracks, and shortley afterwords, all of the cruisers had to have locking gun racks and cages in all.

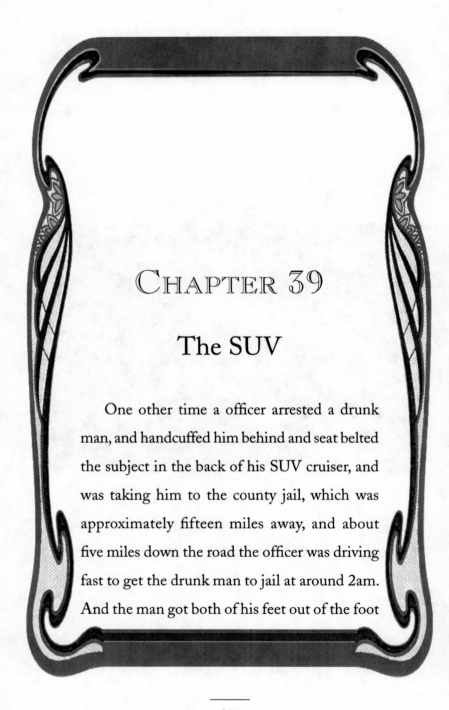

CHAPTER 39

The SUV

One other time a officer arrested a drunk man, and handcuffed him behind and seat belted the subject in the back of his SUV cruiser, and was taking him to the county jail, which was approximately fifteen miles away, and about five miles down the road the officer was driving fast to get the drunk man to jail at around 2am. And the man got both of his feet out of the foot restraints and started kicking the officer in his right shoulder, and before the officer could get stopped, "unknown to the officer at that time his shoulder was dislocated in the altercation" the man was restrained again and the officer proceded to take him to jail.

And later the officer had to retired early do to the fact he has lost most of the use of his arm.

Another sisutation that had happened in another branch of are department and while a national police show was filming and was riding with the officer in his cruiser, and this one night the officer had got behind a drunk driver who had ran a stop sign, and called in pursuit of the said vehicle, and the vehicle kept going faster and faster, going through red lights in the populated area, and reached very high speeds, and the filming crew in the cruiser getting it all on film, a camera mans dream, and about ten minutes into the pursuit up ahead there was a subject in a regular size car with a subject setting at a red light, and the pursued vehicle coming directley toward the stopped vehicle.

And in a mater of seconds the vehicle struck the stopped vehicle in the rear at a high rate of speed, and the person in the stopped vehicle had expired up on impact, and the drunk man was taken to the hospital, and later to jail, and that brought the police department a tougher pursuit policy.

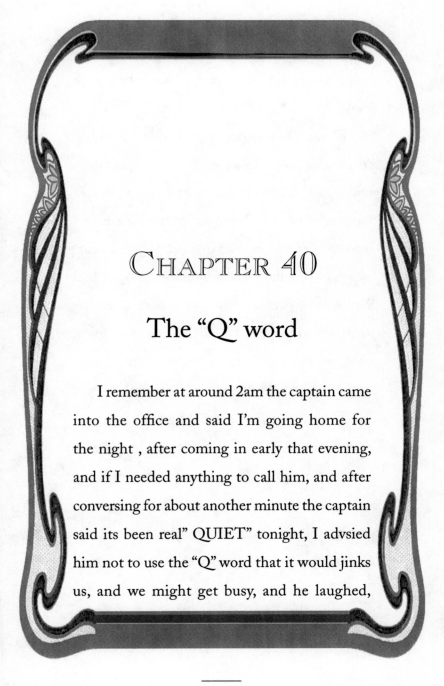

Chapter 40

The "Q" word

I remember at around 2am the captain came into the office and said I'm going home for the night , after coming in early that evening, and if I needed anything to call him, and after conversing for about another minute the captain said its been real" QUIET" tonight, I advsied him not to use the "Q" word that it would jinks us, and we might get busy, and he laughed, and almost as if it had been planed the phone rang.

It was a fire alarm at a Chemical building in are area , and I responed the fire department and a two other officers, and when one officer went into the building they found a man and also noticed that he had open and spilled some type of Chemical, and not knowing what had happened two other officers responded, and the man was arrested, and do to the type of chemical that was in the air, and exposure, to the subject and some of the officers, the Chemical units of E M S and Fire Department had the man who was arrested and had to strip off all his clothes, and go through a washing process before being taken to the hospital to be checked out, also some of the officers who were involved had to go through the same process, which I'm sure would be a very humbling experience for anyone.

Later after speaking with the Captain whom I had to called out three times that night, advised me he would never use the "Q" word again at work.

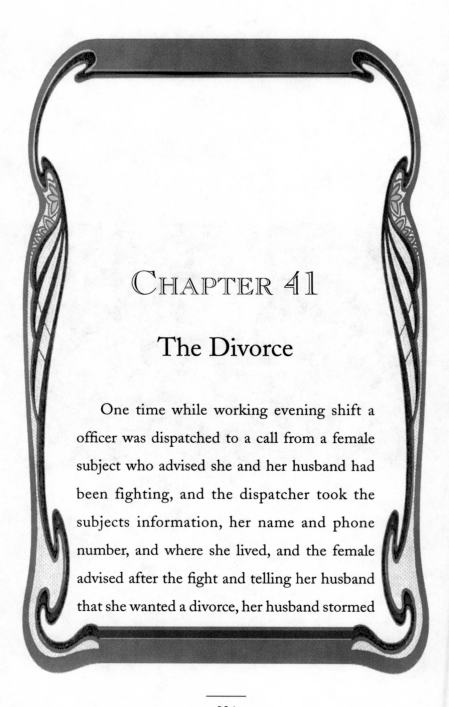

CHAPTER 41

The Divorce

One time while working evening shift a officer was dispatched to a call from a female subject who advised she and her husband had been fighting, and the dispatcher took the subjects information, her name and phone number, and where she lived, and the female advised after the fight and telling her husband that she wanted a divorce, her husband stormed out of the house in there black pickup truck, and took his handgun with him and advised he was going to kill himself, after giving the officer the direction of travel and location where the subject lived, the officer was in the area looking for the vehicle.

After about a half an hour, the officer spotted the vehicle in question, and ran his plate and after following him he turned on his over head flashing lights and pulled the subject over, and when the officer got out of his cruiser, the male subject also got out of his car, and when the officer started to walk toward the man, the man put the revolver to his head and pulled the trigger.Another incident where a officer had to deal with what he had witnessed and try to wipe it out of his mind in getting ready for the next call.

And as I've said before one of the most dangerous sisituations for a police officer to be in is dealing with a person who is threating to kill him or her self, because if they will take there own life they would have nothing to loose to take someone else with them.

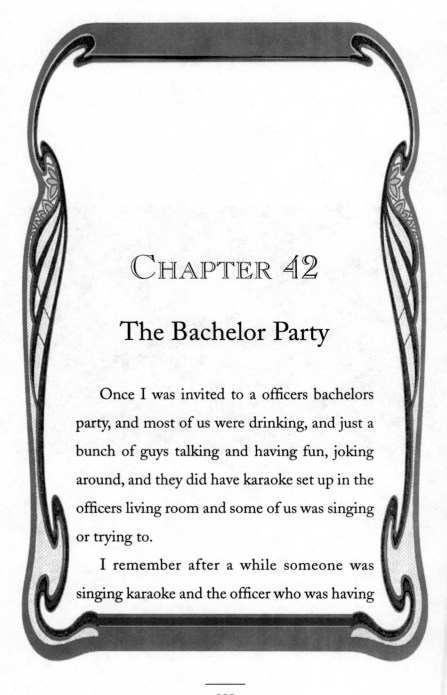

CHAPTER 42

The Bachelor Party

Once I was invited to a officers bachelors party, and most of us were drinking, and just a bunch of guys talking and having fun, joking around, and they did have karaoke set up in the officers living room and some of us was singing or trying to.

I remember after a while someone was singing karaoke and the officer who was having the party walked by the person singing and sprayed pepper spray into the air, and the next thing I knew we all were out side the residence sneezing and caughing and that broke up the party, and a far as I know the officer is still maried.

Another time a officer would spray a little pepper spray in someones work area, so when the officer would sat down to do his or her report , they would inhale the spray that remained in the area, and some would use pepper spray to unclog there own sinuses by spraying a little on there finger and smell there finger. "not a reckemended cure".

Another little known trick some of the officers would do with pepper spray, after going to a residence and knocking on the door to serve a warrant, they could hear someone go to the door but was pretending not to be at home, and the officer knowing that the subject was on the other side of the door sprayed pepper mace under the door and the subject would most of the time caugh or grunt and the officer at that time would advised the subject ot open the door and they would and the warrant would be served.

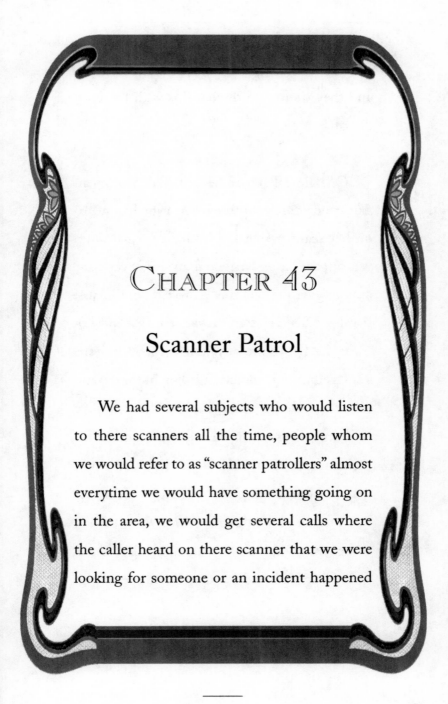

CHAPTER 43

Scanner Patrol

We had several subjects who would listen to there scanners all the time, people whom we would refer to as "scanner patrollers" almost everytime we would have something going on in the area, we would get several calls where the caller heard on there scanner that we were looking for someone or an incident happened and they wanted to discuss this with the busy dispatcher.

One time I remember a female calling in from one of are counties advised she had heard on her scanner that her husbands registration was ran and he was a good man and never done anything wrong ever, and I advsied her that just becaused his registration was ran, that did not mean he had done anything wrong, and she kept yelling and defending her husband and said, thats not right, and I advised her that if an off duty officer was in the area he might get his registration ran, and If I was in the area I might get mine ran aswell, and the officer working the area might be looking for a vehicle thats simular to her husbands vehicle, and she still was not satified, so I advised her to call and speak with the sergeant in that area, and I'm not sure if she did or not, I did not hear back from her again.

Other times we would have someone who had heard on there scanners that someone was missing or escapee in are area, and everytime they saw a person walking in the neighborhood, that in there minds would be the person that the police was looking for.

And also some subjects after listening to information they had heard on the scanner they would call in and try to get information from the dispatcher as to what was going on, also TV and Radio stations had there own aledged scanner patrollers, and would call in and try to obtain information not yet ready for the public, most of the time being a car accident where someone was possibly dead, or a shooting that had happened in the area, and of course we could not release any information until the officer had instructed us to do so.

In all a dispatcher had to put up with dealing with calls coming in on all the phone lines, and giving out calls to the officers on the road, and at the same time deal with scanner patrollers who was just enquiring information, if they had any idea how busy we were, they would never call in unless they had something to really report, some had way too much time on there hands.

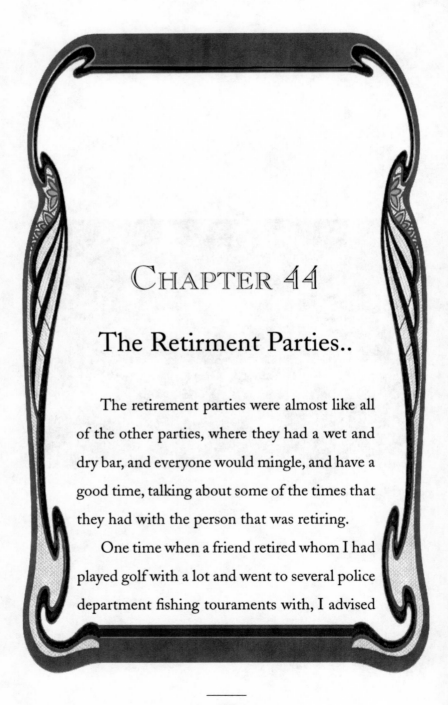

CHAPTER 44

The Retirment Parties..

The retirement parties were almost like all of the other parties, where they had a wet and dry bar, and everyone would mingle, and have a good time, talking about some of the times that they had with the person that was retiring.

One time when a friend retired whom I had played golf with a lot and went to several police department fishing touraments with, I advised him that it had been nice to have been aquainted with him and that we had some great times together, and he advised me he was not dieing but just retiring, and I advised him, I knew that but it seems like when someone retires they disapear, and you never see they again.

Also they had a live local country band there and knowing that I did Elvis impersonations, I was ask to do a Elvis song, so I used one of the bands guitars and advised that I was going to do this song for the officer who was a great friend and who was retiring.

Afterwords I shook hands with the officer and left and maybe seen him once or twice and then he ended up taking another job in another city and moved away, and as I had perdicted, we lost contact with each other.

Another party was when a Captain had retired, and his retirement party was about one hundred miles away, so me and my girlfriend Roberta had to stay over night in that city, so we got a room, and at the party, they had a very large grill set up with all the steak you could eat, they also had a wet and dry bar, and also karaoke, and a DJ, and a dance floor, and after saying are farewells, I also lost contact with him and never saw him again.

CHAPTER 45

Overall View

As an overall view of my career as a dispatcher, from the old school of the way of dispatching police officers to the new school way of dispatching, it's been a trip. From dealing with all types of complaints, from bad weather to domestics, auto accidents, and from irate people to worried mothers and fathers etc., I've seen it all; and I've worked with some of the best people ever, for the most part, and I've enjoyed dispatching for state police, the city police, and even some for the US Forest Service during a Rainbow meeting in one of our counties and Department of Natural Resources (DNR), and dispatching for the university police department in our area—overall twenty-six years of experience.

In the early years, when dispatchers and police officers were hired, they had to go through a background investigation, and the police departments trusted each and every worker; we had no TV cameras overlooking our workplace, and we felt trusted in that position. In the same respect, it seems like today, even though the departments still do extensive checks on all prior to hiring, with all the recordings, TV cams, and scrutiny, as a worker I really don't feel fully trusted, and others whom I have worked with feel the same way, so I guess I miss being trusted like I was in the old school of law enforcement.

I've made a lot of friends, and I hope to leave behind a legacy and hope to be remembered for more than just being another radio operator or dispatcher.

I hope that everyone who reads this book will find it informational, funny, and will somewhat understand how things were in the old days versus how the way things are today in the law enforcement world. If anyone has any comment after reading this book, feel free to contact me at swickstar@yahoo.com

The End

LaVergne, TN USA
29 March 2011
222067LV00004B/127/P